SUTTON, Sarah

Relax and make your
stress work for you

Relax

and make your stress work for you

Sarah Sutton

The 7 Step Plan

BBC ACTIVE

BBC Active, an imprint of Educational Publishers LLP, part of the
Pearson Education Group
Edinburgh Gate
Harlow
Essex CM20 2JE
England

First published in 2006 by BBC Active

ISBN-10: 0-563-52001-9
ISBN-13: 978-0-563-52001-6

Commissioning Editor: Emma Shackleton
Project Editor: Helena Caldon
Text Designer: Annette Peppis
Cover Designer: Annette Peppis
Production Controller: Man Fai Lau

Printed and bound by Ashford Colour Press Ltd, UK

The Publisher's policy is to use paper manufactured from
sustainable forests.

Contents

Acknowledgements

The content of this book draws heavily on the knowledge and expertise of the stress management professionals who contributed to the learning materials in the following BBC business training packs: *20 Steps to Better Management*; *The Pressure's On*; *Putting Stress to Work*; *Managing Time*; *Say the Right Thing*. My role has been to distil and interpret their approach for the general reader.

With grateful thanks to: all those who passed on their personal stories and stress-management strategies; Emma Shackleton, inspired commissioning editor and publisher; Annette Peppis and Helena Caldon, for their talent. With special thanks to Revd Judith Roberts, Dr Pat Tate, the Sutton family and KK.

Preface
Managing 'the last straw'

'It is not stress that kills us. It is our reaction to it.'

HANS SELYE (MD, DSC, PHD), STRESS PIONEER AND AUTHOR OF *THE STRESS OF LIFE* (1956)

S tress. The word itself hisses with tension and jangles abruptness. We can't avoid stress and we can't live without it, but if we can learn to manage its causes we can learn to manage its effects too.

If you have picked up this book it's likely that the effects of stress are causing you concern – either because pressures in your own life mean that you are currently out of balance, or because you are aware of the impact that undue stress is having on someone close to you.

The first step towards making a positive difference in such a situation is to recognize that if you are feeling stressed, the pressure is real – you are not making it up. The compulsion to feel that you 'ought' to be coping or that you need to 'pull yourself together' can delay recognizing and dealing with the causes of stress to the point where your attitude can make things worse. Your feelings are personal to you, and your response to a situation is unique, so it is vital to avoid berating yourself for your lack of ability to cope.

In extreme situations, stress can kill. Relentless stress crushes the spirit, destroys confidence, disrupts families, contributes to the development of major illnesses; and in some instances can lead to suicidal thoughts and actions. The Japanese have a word for it: *karoshi*, which literally translated means 'burn-out death'.

However, on the plus side stress can also stimulate: in short bursts it contributes to medal-winning success in sport, increased performance in the workplace, productive multi-tasking in the home and the capacity to 'go the extra mile' to achieve excellence in all aspects of life.

Each individual has an immense capacity to deal with life's pressures; many people will cope, against all odds, with a variety of challenges and will do so with fortitude and determination for considerable lengths of time. It is usually the cumulative nature of stress, rather than the occasional trial, that puts the body and psyche under pressure of collapse. In the end it can be something quite minor that leads to an inability to cope any longer.

The purpose of this book is to enable you to turn negative causes of stress into something more constructive. The ideas within these pages should help you to stop feeling as if the world is against you and instead realize that you can be in control, even when you are overwhelmed; to learn to trust your own abilities and be true to yourself, rather than dancing to the tune of others; to have the guts to 'get tough' on yourself if your pattern is making your situation worse.

Stress is the enemy of potential. The more you feel weighed down, bored or unable to be 'yourself' in any situation, the less able you will be to enjoy life and deliver results that match your capabilities. Everyone has the right to release their potential and to become the best they can be.

Drawing on professional stress-management techniques, the chapters that follow will help you to put together short-term and long-term strategies for coping with pressure and avoiding sources of stress in the home and workplace. But first you need to 'know your enemy' and understand the nature of stress: both what it is and the physical effects it has on the body. Remember the story of the straw that broke the over-laden camel's back? Managing stress means becoming self-aware to the point that you regain control *before* you reach the point of breakdown; that you recognize in advance what your reasonable limits are and you avoid these 'last straw' moments.

Introduction
What is stress?

'In any moment of decision the best thing you can do is the right thing, the next best thing is the wrong thing, and the worst thing you can do is nothing.'

THEODORE ROOSEVELT

Many people are on a life-stress treadmill. They have been stressed for so long that they don't know what 'normal' behaviour is any more. If this applies to you, and you don't act when a moment of crisis awareness breaks through, there is a danger that you will step right back onto the treadmill again without making any changes – until the next time a crisis hits, when the impact will be even greater. Denying the reality of, or doing nothing about your situation won't make it go away – over time it will just get worse.

The difference between pressure and stress

There is a difference between pressure – the forces that act upon us and that we react to – and stress, which is our negative response when pressure gets too great. Pressure is inevitable, and it is also a necessary element in achieving peak performance in life. However, too much pressure can put a strain on the mind, the body and the spirit which can result in negative stress.

Recognizing that there is a difference between

pressure and stress is the first step towards taking back
control of your situation. Reduce or change the pressure
and the stress will diminish.

'I can't go on like this any longer'

In a time-starved world of high demands and deadlines,
you may feel an overwhelming need to halt the mounting
pressure *now*, to turn off the symptoms of anxiety *now*, to
reconnect with your true self and to get your life back on
track, *now*. This book will help you to stop the treadmill
for long enough to realize that things *can* change – and
they can change for the better. The aim of each chapter
is to provide insights and knowledge that will help you to
remind yourself of who you really are; to change the way
you see yourself and your current situation so that you *can*
do things differently and begin to reduce the stress...*now*.

Relax and make your stress work for you will put *you* back
in control; it sits you firmly in the driving seat of your life
and helps you to view personal challenges in a new light,
enabling you to make the most of your unique qualities
and rediscover your individual style. The practical tips,
techniques and action points are designed to increase your
coping skills, to rally you to optimize your potential, and
encourage you to trust your own abilities and develop self-
knowledge.

If personal challenge has turned into personal
overload, it doesn't have to be that way. It may be hard to
believe when you are at your most stressed, but you can
turn these feelings and symptoms of stress into a force for
positive change. Read on, and the choices that you make

from today onwards will gradually make stress a thing of the past.

What is stress?

'Stress, in addition to being itself, [is] also the cause of itself, and the result of itself.'
HANS SELYE

So what exactly do we mean by stress? When does a personal challenge become stressful? When do feelings of anxiety become dangerous? How exactly does stress affect the body – and how can we change its impact from negative to positive?

Stress is an over-used term. It is just as likely to be employed to describe the sense of acute anxiety that is felt when under pressure to complete too many tasks before lunch-time, as it is to be applied to symptoms of deep trauma experienced by a soldier in a war zone, or the chronic exhaustion experienced by a carer who is looking after a highly dependent relative. It is not so much the nature of the situation that drives the experience of stress as the individual's response to it.

The concept of 'stress' was first defined in 1936 by the Hungarian endocrinologist Hans Selye, who used the term to describe the common physical and emotional effects of undue strain on the body. Dr Selye was the first physician to define two types of strain: positive *pressure*, which contributes to feelings of well-being; and negative *stress* which may contribute to illnesses such as heart

Relax and make your stress work for you

disease, cancer, mental disorders and gastric problems. He identified three phases of development, which are still generally accepted today:

The 'alarm' reaction

This is commonly known as the 'fight or flight' syndrome. When faced with a threat, the adrenaline levels in the body increase quickly for a short time while we decide whether to confront the danger or to run away. The body cannot keep up this level of adrenaline production for long, so this phase transforms into:

Resistance or adaptation

This is a deeper version of 'fight or flight' as the body either resists the cause of stress or adapts to it. In this way we adjust to the pressures put upon us, or we avoid them altogether by changing our focus (or job, or lifestyle, etc.). This phase can continue for a long time. If the source of negative stress also continues, without remission, this second stage leads to:

Exhaustion

It is at this point that tiredness or depression start to appear and ever more energy is needed to produce lesser results. It is in this state that a minor event can become 'the last straw' that tips coping behaviour into tearful despair. In this period, the body may become ill or show signs of premature ageing. Something urgently needs to change to prevent this stage developing into personal breakdown.

(See p. 34 for further explanation of how this stress curve affects us.)

Positively stressed

One person's suffering with stress is another's personal challenge and, within reason, stress (in the form of positive pressure) can have a beneficial impact on our lives. We all need challenge and stimulus in order to learn and grow and there are many people who choose to live life at the sharp end because they think and respond best in an adrenaline-fired environment.

Provided the body is strong and healthy it is possible to think sharp, to be effective and to go without sleep for short periods of time with no long-term disadvantage. This is demonstrated by the many students who cram for exams with no adverse effects, in the way the emergency services operate effectively whilst under immense pressure, or by the person who has to prepare for an important presentation at short notice. Conversely, a lack of pressure and the effects of lack of stimulation can actually be debilitating.

However, high levels of pressure can be endured only if the body and mind are healthy: if the extremes of activity are balanced by periods of relaxation and calm, combined with enough sleep and nourishment. The difficulty comes when the extreme pattern of behaviour carries on for too long.

Stress occurs when the demands made on an individual are greater than their ability to cope.

A national epidemic?

In the UK alone tens of thousands of people each year
are diagnosed with stress-related conditions. Recent
research undertaken by the Future Foundation reveals
that 12 million people each week suffer from anxiety-
related insomnia, and one in every 20 people has taken
anti-depressants to help them cope with life's pressures.
Compared with the results of a Gallup poll in 1954 – which
revealed that just 6 in every 100 people believed that
things could get worse during the year ahead – in current
times, nearly 50 per cent of the population anticipates that
they will be worse off by the end of the year, and two out
of every three people believe we are in more danger of a
third world war than ever before. So is it any wonder that
we are feeling stressed?!

How stress-prone are you?

Take a moment to answer the following questions. Answer
them *twice* before checking your scores: first, giving your
responses in a work context and then again giving your
social responses. Is there a difference?

1	Are you casual about appointments?	A
	Are you never late?	B
2	Are you very competitive?	A
	Are you rarely competitive?	B
3	Do you find it easy to listen?	A
	Do you often interrupt?	B

4	Are you always rushed?	A
	Are you never rushed?	B
5	Can you wait patiently?	A
	Are you impatient?	B
6	Do you tend to hide your feelings?	A
	Do you usually express your feelings?	B
7	Do you take things one at a time?	A
	Do you do lots of things at once?	B
8	Would you describe yourself as hard-driving?	A
	Would you describe yourself as easy-going?	B
9	Do you tend to do things slowly (e.g. walking)?	A
	Do you tend to do things quickly (e.g. rushing)?	B
10	Do you have few leisure interests?	A
	Do you have a lot of leisure interests?	B

Scoring

Odd-numbered questions:

Score 2 points for every B you have selected.

Even-numbered questions:

Score 2 points for every A you have selected.

The traits that carry a score are typical of an 'A'-type personality (see p. 23). The higher your score, the more stress you are imposing on yourself. If you score high in both work and leisure time, you are subjecting yourself to double the level of stress.

○ A score of 16 or more shows that you need to take active steps to reduce stress – now. Disregarding this result will have an adverse effect on your health, relationships and quality of life. It is time to change.

❍ A score of 12–16 shows a high degree of motivation and concern about time. You may be putting yourself under stress in the longer term and you should be aware of the warning signs. (See pp. 20 and 28.)

❍ A score of 5–12 suggests you have a fairly relaxed approach. You may not be overly ambitious, but you probably have a balanced attitude to both work and home.

❍ A score of 4 or less suggests either a *laissez-faire* attitude to life or excellent forward planning. Be aware that your low stress could result in increased anxiety for your family, friends or colleagues if they have to pick up the pieces. On the other hand, you may be a master at forward planning and thus avoid stress by being ahead of the game.

Something's got to change

Stress management begins in the mind, with the recognition that something's got to change or that you can't go on this way and your current approach to tackling the demands of life aren't working. Knowing that you need to change is not enough – keep doing what you're doing and you'll keep getting what you've got.

Once you become aware that you are putting yourself at risk you have a choice: you can choose either to ignore the warning signs, or you can value yourself enough to commit to making some changes in your life and your approach to all aspects of it.

The first step to beat stress is to learn how to relax, and how to calm your breathing.

How you can help yourself – step 1: Relax and live

Be aware

Take a moment to be aware of your body. Stress goes hand in hand with tension: it affects the muscles of your face, your neck, your stomach and other organs, and it can make you more prone to injury, depression and premature ageing. If you are suffering the effects of chronic stress at the moment, you're probably displaying a cluster of the following signs:

o Hunched shoulders
o Tightly-crossed legs
o Crossed arms
o Chewed lip
o Neck spasm
o Bowel problems
o Shallow breathing
o Nervous cough
o Furrowed brows
o Clenched fists
o Tight jaw
o Eye twitch
o Lower back pain
o Tension headache
o Incessant yawning

You might be so used to some symptoms that you hadn't even noticed they were there. Start to beat your stress right now by letting go of inner tension and learning to breathe.

Take action
Breathe deeply

o Take a moment now to focus on the aspect of your life that is causing you the most pressure at the present time.
o Notice the emotions that surface and the physical sensations that you feel as you think about it.

○ Place your hands over your diaphragm and take a deep breath.

○ Hold your breath for a count of three and then breathe out, slowly and fully.

○ The out-breath needs to be longer than the in-breath in order to achieve calmness.

○ Breathe in again. Hold your breath for a count of three, then breathe out, slowly and fully.

○ Repeat the process at least three to five times.

○ Concentrate on your breathing and feel the intake of air refreshing your body and your mind.

○ If you are still feeling upset or tense, continue with this exercise – whatever your emotional state – until you feel your breathing becoming calmer.

○ As your breathing calms, so you will feel calmer.

Commit to change

There is immense power in this simple exercise. Use it several times each day, and especially during periods when you are feeling overwhelmed, angry or tearful. By this simple process you are changing your body's physical response to stress and thereby altering your emotional state as well.

The key to managing stress is the ability to control your emotional state. Once you can do this you will be in a strong position to influence your behaviour and your responses to the pressures that you are facing.

1 Stress and you
Understanding your response to stress

'What we think, or what we know, or what we believe is, in the end, of little consequence. The only consequence is what we do.'

JOHN RUSKIN

You are most likely to feel stress when the pressure has built to a level where you feel out of control: when you have too much to do and not enough time to do it in; you are overcommitted; physically or mentally exhausted; ill or bereaved; or when you are spending so much time focused on the needs of others that you have lost track of your own.

A life of stress?

There have been huge changes in our lifestyle in recent years and modern life now puts us all under pressure from many sources. Of course, the two most common culprits for creating stress in our lives tend to be work and home:

At work: Far from making life easier, modern technology has actually sped things up so much that we now receive more information more quickly, and as a result we are expected to react to it faster than ever before. Most companies have also been streamlined in recent years, which in turn has put greater pressure on both permanent employees and freelancers. No one has job security in today's workplace, and 50 per cent of the population is lacking a pension. We also work longer hours in the UK than anywhere else in Europe – although we are not necessarily more productive.

At home: We are spending less time in the home and with our children than previous generations, because being a stay-at-home parent is not an option if there are bills to pay. And yet the household chores still need to be done. The extended family is often spread further afield nowadays, which means a different style of visiting and involvement that makes it difficult for families to provide support to those who need it.

In addition, the western world is now very materialistic and there is great pressure to possess material goods and to go away on holiday. This stress factor, of course, is inextricably linked to pressures at work, in that we need to earn sufficient money to be able to achieve and maintain our chosen lifestyle.

How we respond to the pressures of work and home depends largely upon our individual personality and whether or not we have an effective support network. However, for ease of analysis psychologists tend to divide people broadly into two groups:

'A'-type personalities are more likely to rush about, show competitive traits and be perfectionists. This is the group that is most prone to constant stress. (Revisit the questionnaire on p. 17 to see whether you fall into this category.)

'B'-type personalities take a more balanced approach, are more easy-going and cope better with short-term stress – but they are equally prone to suffering stress if they feel out of control or over-pressured.

To understand your own personal response to stress, learning to recognize your own stress-points so that you can take preventative action is crucial. In order to do this, give yourself some time to take stock of how you live and to analyze your support network. If you are leading a stressful existence, the chances are that your friends or family will notice your stress before you do. They will pick up on any changes in your appearance, your mood, your responses, your eating, drinking or smoking habits, your health, or the increase in your excuses for why you can't do certain things: 'I can't because...I'm working/I'm looking after the kids/I'm broke/my mother needs me/I've got too much to do/I'm just too exhausted ...'

If you have been functioning at maximum capacity without a break over several weeks or months, there is a fine line between needing space to unwind at the end of a hard day and feeling so chronically stressed that you can't cope with having company at all. This is exactly what happened to Ray, in a scenario that is being played out in thousands of households in different ways every day:

Case study: Identifying stress

*Ray had been promoted to a senior management role in a
demanding sales environment; a job made more challenging by
the fact that it was in a town too far from home to commute to on
a daily basis. So Ray had to live away from his wife and children
during the week and went home only at weekends. Six months in,
he was getting to grips with his new role, but he was permanently
exhausted. He had no time or inclination to get to know people
locally, not least because he was working long hours every day
and an increasing number of weekends. This in turn meant that
his trips home were few and far between, so he was seeing less
and less of his family and old friends.*

*Although Ray lived alone during the week, he did not
consider himself lonely. He had no reason to suspect that he wasn't
coping with his new lifestyle until his wife, Amy, came to stay for
a week without the children. She was shocked by his lethargy, the
state of his home from home, and his new drinking habits.*

*Realizing that he was neglecting himself, Amy prepared
meals for him to eat when he returned home late from work.
Instead of appreciating her kindness, Ray found himself snapping
unreasonably and being highly ungrateful, and on one occasion
he suggested that she should stop fussing and leave. It was an
extreme and negative response to a kind and loving gesture, and
a distressing experience for both of them. From then on, Amy gave
him a wide berth when he first arrived home, 'until you've had
time to relax'.*

*Ray conjectures: 'It was quite an eye-opener for me. I hadn't
realized how wound up I was when I got in at night. When I was
on my own during the week my true mood was hidden because
I wasn't talking to anybody. I had got into the habit of cracking*

open a bottle of wine, grabbing a takeaway, watching TV and avoiding the phone. There was an illusion of coping but, in fact, I wasn't coping at all. Having Amy to stay made me realize that I was behaving out of character and that we needed to do something to get our life as a family back in balance.'

Stress and your health

Stress has a cumulative effect on the whole person – in physical as well as emotional ways – and that is why a stress response can sometimes appear to be out of all proportion to the event that triggered it. However, what seems to be a relatively small event can often be the last straw.

Sources of stress

Increased pressure over time can produce a constant variety of ever-changing, and sometimes contradictory, stress symptoms. When analyzing your current situation, consider how many of these sources of stress feature in your life.

❍ Work overload: Having insufficient resources to complete task/s in the time necessary, or constantly over-committing personal time.
❍ Under-stimulation: Lack of a personal challenge or being without work can cause frustration, anger or lethargy.
❍ Task avoidance: Self-inflicted stress caused by procrastination, poor time management or lack of effective prioritization.
❍ Crisis management: Caused by constantly changing priorities.

❍ Long-term care of a family member, bereavement or
divorce: Feelings of grief, exacerbated by administrative
pressures.

❍ Home, family or social pressures: Financial pressures,
relationship issues, or concern for those in your care.

❍ Poor communication: Not being involved in or consulted
about decisions that will affect you; a sense of not knowing
what is going on.

❍ The inability to say 'no': Poor delegation or an inability
to put your own needs first.

❍ Lack of sleep: Chronic fatigue, related health problems
and lack of concentration.

❍ Lack of recognition for work done well.

❍ Environmental stress from excessive noise, smells or
other external problems.

❍ Personality: An inherent tendency to be anxious,
depressive, obsessional, or excitable. Lack of self-esteem.

❍ Lack of planning: A tendency to drift can lead to anxiety
and crisis management.

❍ Perfectionism: The inability to delegate or to finish and
let go of a task. An ongoing sense of disappointment.

❍ Small innocuous events: The ones that feel like the last
straw.

The good news is that positive change is possible. The
causes of stress may be varied and outside our immediate
control, but our ability to deal with its effects lies within
our mind and with our emotions.

Managing stress is about acquiring self-knowledge. In order not to reach breaking point we need to learn how to see stress coming, to understand our personal stress trigger points and our own responses to stress – and we need to believe that we can bring about positive change in such situations.

On their own, some symptoms of stress are fairly innocuous; however, clusters of symptoms combined and experienced over a long period of time can have a profound and draining effect on our ability to function efficiently.

Common symptoms of stress
Physical
○ Sudden headaches
○ The inability to relax or sleep properly
○ Stiff neck and shoulders
○ Extreme fatigue
○ Gastro-intestinal problems including constipation, indigestion and diarrhoea
○ Loss of appetite
○ Palpitations
○ Rapid pulse
○ Butterflies in your stomach
○ Tightness in the stomach or chest
○ Breathing difficulties
○ Cold, clammy hands
○ Trembling hands
○ Dry mouth
○ Anxiety attacks
○ Feeling faint

- Memory problems
- Skin problems
- Menstrual problems

Emotional

- Feelings of helplessness
- Feeling out of control
- Constantly feeling tense or 'wound up'
- Tiredness and apathy
- Tearfulness or anger
- Irritability or aggressiveness
- Low self-esteem and lack of confidence

Behavioural

- Procrastination
- Perfectionism
- Tendency to talk fast
- Need to be constantly productive
- Inability to concentrate
- Being fidgety
- Indecisiveness
- Tendency to be short-tempered or critical
- Overreaction to trivial things
- Introversion and need to be solitary
- Escapist eating or drinking
- Increase in accidents or physical injuries

Recognizing your stress symptoms may not make you feel any better about having them – but it is the first stage on your return to a more balanced lifestyle.

How stress affects the body

We all know what we mean when we say that we are stressed, but in order to understand and overcome its effects we also need to understand how stress actually impacts on the body. Feelings of stress or excitement trigger immediate physical and chemical changes in the body that are designed to help us to cope with and adapt to the source of the stress or excitement, or to escape from it. Amazingly, exactly the same chemical response is triggered by danger as by nervous excitement.

The following sections give a brief explanation of how the body responds to stress. Some people find that having a basic understanding of the body's response helps ease their feelings of panic and fear. The state of nervous tension is not permanent – it can be managed and it will pass.

The nervous system

The nervous system is made up of the brain, the spinal cord, nerves and nervous tissue and we use it to interpret information about the outside world via our senses: taste, touch, sight, smell and hearing.

The nervous system operates automatically and is made up of two parts. Both systems supply the same organs of the body, but they create opposite effects: the *parasympathetic* nervous system is concerned with long-term survival, whereas the *sympathetic* nervous system is concerned with short-term survival.

The parasympathetic nervous system directs blood to your digestive system to make sure you digest food and keeps your blood pressure, heart rate and breathing at a low level. It also sustains and restores your energy levels after a period of threat.

The sympathetic nervous system drives the 'fight or flight' response that you have to a stressful or dangerous situation and prepares the body for emergency action. It converts the energy stored by the parasympathetic nervous system into immediately usable energy, which is stored only for short periods.

When we are threatened – by danger, challenge, or anything that causes us anxiety – the brain stimulates the sympathetic nervous system and the pituitary gland to switch the body's resources from long-term to short-term survival. Once this is done, everything is then optimized to overcome the immediate threat.

The stress hormones

So when we reach a point of stress the hormones adrenaline and noradrenaline (which control this 'fight or flight' response) spring into action, are released into the body and trigger the major changes needed to prepare the relevant organs and muscles for emergency action or a fast getaway. This effect goes something like this:

○ Blood drains away from our extremities (hands and feet).
○ The stomach begins to increase the supply of stress hormones to our brain and vital organs, causing a sensation of 'butterflies' in the stomach.
○ The heart starts to beat faster and blood pressure rises.

❍ Our breathing changes.
❍ Muscles tense, ready for action.

The most powerful of these so-called stress hormones is cortisol. Cortisol is responsible for keeping fat and sugar at high levels in the bloodstream in order to provide instant energy, and its level of production increases in response to any stress in the body – whether physical or psychological. When an increase in cortisol is needed, messages are sent via the brain to the pituitary gland. Once the levels are high enough, a reverse message is sent and the production is reduced.

The physical changes that this hormone stimulates prepare the heart and lungs for emergency action and tense the muscles for fight or flight. The response is the same whether faced with real danger, such as a motorway collision, or simply with a situation where you are feeling 'wound up': for example, when stuck in a queue or a traffic jam; when faced with a telephone call-waiting system; or when forced to listen to a complaining neighbour. If the 'fight' impulse is restrained there is nowhere for the tension to go, and it is at this point that we are in danger of 'losing it'.

Under normal circumstances, once the threat has passed, the parasympathetic nervous system comes back into action to reverse the effect of the 'fight or flight' response and to restore the body's energy levels to 'long-term' survival mode. However, in periods of chronic pressure (that is, pressure that continues, unrelentingly, for many weeks or months), the body has no opportunity to replenish its energy levels. If the 'fight or flight' response is constantly being triggered, we eventually reach a point where we can no longer sustain the imbalance in our body chemistry and we become exhausted. In this situation the body calls an 'emergency' state and starts to use up its resources of vitamin C, the B vitamins, magnesium and zinc and increases oxidation damage. Chronic stress, therefore, reduces the efficiency of the immune system – which is why when we are stressed we become more susceptible to infections, our skin loses its healthy glow and we are prone to headaches, raised blood pressure and infections.

If you know that you have a pattern of high stress levels, or suspect that you are entering a period of increased pressure, you need to 'shape up for stress'. (See Chapter 3 for practical suggestions of how to do this and how to keep yourself in a state of stress-resistant good health.)

Entering the stress 'zone'

Stress is experienced through five different pressure/performance 'zones' as explained by Stephen Williams, in his book *Managing Pressure for Peak Performance*. Any of these zones can prove difficult to manage or may be an opportunity for positive change, depending on personal resources and expectations. Our performance level is highest when we are stretched to our maximum, but it dips as soon as we are overstretched to the point where we are straining to keep up with the pressures put upon us. The zones are:

1 Boredom   Skills under-utilized.
2 Comfort   Stuck in a 'comfort zone'.
3 Stretch   Challenged to a degree that you can manage.
4 Strain   Challenged beyond the ability to cope.
5 Panic   At breaking point.

○ Levels 1 and 2 have their challenges, but the stress levels are usually manageable.
○ Level 3 is the one to aim for.
○ Levels 4 and 5 are serious conditions and can lead to mental burnout and physical breakdown.

Psychologists often use a performance curve to show the clear connections between levels of pressure, our ability to cope with it, and the quality of personal performance.

The pressure/performance stages

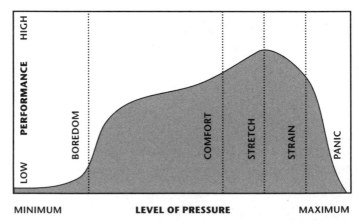

(Source: *The Pressure's On* p. 56.)

Relax and make your stress work for you

The boredom zone

If you are bored and under-stimulated you may lack the motivation to grow and develop. Although you may have little external pressure, the symptoms of negative stress may develop as the result of disappointment or frustration.

To move out of the boredom zone

Identify ways that you can stretch yourself mentally and physically. Set yourself personal goals and take practical steps to achieve them. Watch your mindset – if negative thinking has become a habit, endeavour to turn the negative into positive (see p. 111).

The comfort zone

The comfort zone is a stage in a learning process where things are familiar. This may relate to being satisfied with a level of competence at work, with a social situation, or being comfortable in a routine or with life in general. At this level we are content and can manage whatever comes our way – although there may be some feelings of dissatisfaction relating to lack of growth, stimulation, or overall achievement.

To move out of the comfort zone

Be *consciously* comfortable in order to avoid the tendency to drift into boredom. Don't resist challenge and change and be aware of where you are with your long-term objectives.

Case study: From comfort zone to stretch zone

Russell was a town planner who worked in the public sector. He had joined his local authority after qualifying at the age of 25, was married at 29 and by the age of 42, although a little bored, was comfortable in his community and routine and was satisfied that he had made sensible decisions about salary, security and pension.

Russell had always met his performance targets and got on well with colleagues, but he had never been promoted to senior management because he was always happy to let others take the strain. However, he had recently received a negative annual appraisal that drew attention to his lack of ambition and he was now under pressure to move sideways to allow others to progress, or to 'bite the bullet' and take on a senior post.

Russell was filled with anxiety about the potential forthcoming changes – fearful that he would not be able to adjust to managing those he had worked alongside for so long, but also resentful that a younger subordinate might be promoted above him. He began suffering nervous headaches, started to drink more than usual and developed insomnia.

However, he decided to apply for promotion 'just to see what happens'. This process of applying for the job forced Russell to take stock of his career to date, to do an audit of his personal skills and to see himself as someone who had the maturity and experience to take on a more demanding role. By the time the interview date arrived, he felt a new level of enthusiasm and was looking forward to the challenge – aware that irrespective of whether he got the role, it was time that he started to stretch himself.

The stretch zone

This zone represents a healthy level of stress – where external stimulus encourages personal growth, learning and development. However, there is a balance that needs to be maintained. We continue to learn and grow as long as we are able to manage external pressures effectively, but if we become overstretched, if the learning continues unabated at too great a pace, or if we are subjected to other people's stress, the negative effects of stress will develop and chronic stretch will become strain.

To stay in balance in the stretch zone

Planning and review are the keys to managing the stretch zone, whether you are being stretched at home or at work. You can know where you are in a situation only if you know how far you've travelled. (See Chapter 3 for guidelines on effective planning and review.)

The strain zone

Strain on the body is the result of experiencing the chronic effects of being overstretched for a long period of time. Symptoms of stress may begin to appear (see p. 20) and productivity is likely to diminish, along with personal motivation and interest in things going on around you. You may also notice an increase in fatigue and a desire to retreat from the world.

To move out of the strain zone

To leave the strain zone you need to make time to take stock. If you have been in a stressed state for a while, you will probably need some objective help in order to get a constructive result – you might be so used to your current state of mind that you are unable to envisage life any other way.

Case study: From strain zone to stretch zone

Susan was over the moon when she became a mother at the age of 28. She had worked full-time since leaving school at the age of 18, but after the birth of her daughter, Zoë, she and her partner Carl agreed that she would be a stay-at-home mum until Zoë was old enough to go to school.

Zoë was a delightful baby and, even though her arrival provided plenty of extra work, Susan enjoyed her new role with enthusiasm for the first year. However, by the time Zoë was in the throes of the 'terrible twos' Susan was finding it hard to cope. Her partner's job took him away from home a lot, Zoë was proving to be quite a handful and Susan felt increasingly isolated and out of control. The situation at home began to undermine her confidence and she could feel herself losing her self-esteem. As a result, she became short-tempered and tired and put on a lot of weight.

Susan also worried that by being out of the workplace she was becoming unemployable, and she felt guilty that she seemed unable to cope with tasks that other mothers handled with ease. She felt she couldn't confide in anyone, she craved the ordered environment of the office and she missed the stimulus of adult conversation during the day. Lack of sleep was contributing to the onset of panic attacks and she was becoming intolerant of Zoë's toddler habits. Carl was frequently on the receiving end of Susan's stress-related behaviour and the situation was starting to threaten their relationship.

Near to the brink of separation, they finally began to discuss the situation more seriously. Susan started to realize that many of her fears were both false and self-limiting and that many of her problems with Zoë stemmed from her own unhappiness and their inconsistent parenting. They discussed achieving a balanced lifestyle whereby Susan would give Zoë some home care but would also be able to return to work.

Susan applied to her former employer for a part-time role and used her new income to fund a childminder and pay for a regular yoga class. In less than three months Susan had returned to her former self and had become a positive parent again. Although still lacking sleep and anxious on occasion, she had developed coping strategies – including being more open with Carl about her feelings, and recognizing that she could be a good mother as well as going to work.

The panic zone

When we are in the panic zone we are well aware that we are not coping, but we may be unaware of much else. At this level there is imminent danger of damage to self (or others) both physically and psychologically, because the smallest trigger can tip the balance from reasoned behaviour to being emotionally out of control. The danger of panic is that it leads to impulsive or extreme behaviour that may not be to our best advantage, and in this state we are at a greater risk of breakdown and illness.

To avoid or move out of the panic zone

You need to STOP – at least long enough to change your current frame of mind. In an acute situation, learn to use relaxation techniques (see p. 20) to change your breathing; move away from the situation that is causing you stress; take a break or go for a walk.

If the sense of panic is with you all the time, then you really need to take steps now to make changes to your current situation. No matter how desperate things may seem, you *can* put yourself back in control of things, at least to some extent. (See Chapters 4 and 5 for guidance on speaking out and planning for change.)

Those who are in the panic state are the people who are closest to experiencing breakdown: a dramatic and painful way of stopping the strain. While some may argue that breakdown is a transformational experience in the long term, in the short term it is generally traumatic and painful. You owe it to yourself to get back from the brink if

A summary of the effects of the five different pressu

	Short-term effect
Boredom	Stagnation and lethargy.
	Possible motivation to stretch.
Comfort	Balance and contentment.
Stretch	Anxiety and positive stress.
	Growth and learning, leading to
	either comfort or strain.
Strain	Stress symptoms.
Panic	Fear. Loss of control. 'Fight or flight'.
	Extreme emotions.

at all possible. (See Chapter 7 for guidelines on what to do
if you're feeling out of control.)

Avoiding pressure

The good news is that stress does not have to be the
inevitable consequence of pressure. The key to avoiding
this is to focus on tackling the sources of the pressure
rather than the symptoms of stress. So, try to:

○ Find ways of changing your perception of a situation.
○ Learn and use techniques and practices such as
relaxation and breathing which will ease pressure on
the body.
○ Avoid turning to alcohol or any other stimulants as
a remedy – they will only put the body under even
greater pressure.

erformance 'zones':

Long-term effect

Negative stress symptoms caused by discontent or
lack of stimulus result in strain and panic.

Lack of growth leads to boredom or motivation to stretch.

Negative stress symptoms caused by exhaustion
and lack of balance may lead to strain and panic.

Illness, depression, leading to 'burnout' and panic.

Breakdown. A catalyst for dramatic change.

How you can help yourself – step 2: Face your fears and visualize the future

Be aware

Identify the causes of your stress

Take a little time out to think about how you are feeling, the symptoms of your stress, and what it is that you think causes you stress.

○ Have those around you been commenting on your work pattern, behaviour or physical health?

○ Do you suffer from a cluster of the symptoms listed in this chapter?

○ Is the cause of your stress rooted in your home life, your work, your self-image, or the problems of another person or persons who are dependent upon you?

○ Is the source of the stress new, or have events been chipping away at you for some time?

○ How would you like your life or situation to be different?

○ In what ways would you like your life or situation to remain the same?

○ What are the factors you feel that you can change?

○ What are the factors you feel that you can't change?

These may seem obvious questions to ask yourself, but often when we are under stress a sense of powerlessness stops us taking stock of our personal needs. The pace or magnitude of the pressures you are experiencing may be such that there seems to be no time for 'you', and your anxiety may be making it impossible to think straight or regain control.

Take action

One of the most effective ways to manage stress is to bring order into your sense of chaos by naming and listing the factors that are causing you distress. You owe it to yourself and those around you to treat yourself fairly and to achieve a sense of balance in your life.

○ Put aside a minimum of half an hour at a time when you will be relaxed (for example, after a hot bath or shower, or following a workout at the gym), and take stock of your situation.

○ Arm yourself with a quantity of blank paper and something to write with and find a comfortable and quiet place in which to think and work.

○ Using the questions above as a starting point, 'brainstorm' your reactions to your current situation: your feelings about it, your disappointments, the people that influence you (whether positive or negative) and the factors that have led you to this point – taking into consideration their short- and long-term ramifications.

There are many ways of doing this exercise – you can use Mind Maps®, lists, pictures, spider diagrams, thought-bubbles or doodles. It really doesn't matter how you get the information onto paper; what is important is that you give the process your full attention.

Bringing order into a chaotic life is an intensely personal process, and the thoughts are likely to flow relatively fast once you start working on your list. Don't try to edit them or slow the process down by attempting to present the information in a controlled way: there will be time for that later. Use a combination of words and pictures to stimulate both the creative and logical parts of your brain.

You may find yourself becoming overwhelmed with emotion as your feelings surge to the surface – or be prompted to think about things that surprise you or appear to be outside your current scenario. No matter how the exercise makes you feel, please try to complete it – don't stop the process or be deterred from your task, and try to capture as much information as possible.

Tony Buzan in *Embracing Change* looks at this process in more detail. He encourages you to examine the whole situation and to consider:

❍ The facts of the matter.

❍ Your feelings about it.

❍ Your choices of action.

Once you have sketched out the entire scenario and you feel that you have completed the process, pause to change your mood. You may feel quite weary, so go for a walk, go to sleep, listen to some music, watch TV or make a phone call. Your mind needs time to absorb what you have uncovered.

Commit to change

Now that you have given physical form to the causes of your stress, you'll be able to start realizing your potential by regaining control of your life.

Look at what you have just expressed and identify the thing that is putting you under the most pressure and that you would change if you could. There is usually one main aspect that is driving everything else, and by focusing all your attention on resolving or managing the core issue, the other factors will gradually fall into place.

For example:

○ The decision to stay in a job that you don't enjoy may be driven by concerns about finance.

○ Unreasonable work pressures may be being endured only because of a need for personal recognition.

○ You might be staying in a relationship that is causing you undue pain because of a fear of the unknown or of being alone.

○ Denying yourself a holiday because of commitment to a dependent relative may be driven by feelings of guilt.

○ Taking work home on a regular basis may be the result of poor management skills, or habit.

Commit to drawing up a plan of action to start managing your core problem. The key to success is to 'start where you are' and to realize that you have more choice and more control than you think.

Stress management
How to change your reactions to stress

'In order that people may be happy in their work, these three things are needed: they must be fit for it; they must not do too much of it; and they must have a sense of success in it.'

JOHN RUSKIN

Stress in mind

No two people will respond to pressure in exactly the same way. For every person who sees a situation as a catastrophe, there is another who sees it as a challenge that can be met: one person experiences it as excessive pressure, the other as a period of personal growth. The degree of pressure exerted may be the same on each person, but the level of stress they actually experience is different, and this attitude and outcome depends upon:

○ Perception of the pressure.

○ Level and type of coping skills.

○ Attitude and personality.

○ The length of time the pressure has continued for.

Wayne Froggatt identifies 'twelve rational principles' to help manage stress. The list on p. 47 draws on these.

Perception of the pressure

Pressure can come from anywhere: home, work, socially,
or even from extended family. It can come from a minor
event or a major incident. If we see ourselves as victims of
'unfair' pressure, we will not cope well. However, if we can
see beyond the immediate pressure to a possible plan or
solution, we will be better equipped to handle the situation
because we have taken control of it.

Level and type of coping skills

We each have coping skills; some are more constructive
than others, and some are downright destructive.

Positive coping skills include:

○ Self-knowledge – an acceptance of who you are right now
and what your strengths and limitations might be.

○ Self-confidence in your skills, in your ability to handle
the situation and in your ability to change (if you choose
to, and if necessary).

○ A healthy self-interest in your ability to problem-solve,
coupled with sufficient self-respect to believe in your right
to a positive outcome.

○ A reasonable level of tolerance – the ability to cope with
a degree of discomfort or frustration with the situation,
or to cope with disliking the attitudes of other people
involved without losing your cool and without feeling the
need to avoid them.

○ A reasonable level of risk-taking that will enable you
to learn new skills, tackle tasks that have no guarantee of
success, and to try new relationships.

○ The ability to laugh and a sense of the absurd.

Negative avoidance skills include:

○ Bombarding the senses by indulging in the excesses of drinking, smoking or recreational drugs, binge-eating, credit-card shopping or casual sex.

○ Adopting a 'victim' mentality: thinking 'poor me', 'it's not fair' and assuming that everyone else has an easier life.

○ Apportioning blame: 'it's not my fault', 'it's someone else's fault', to avoid taking personal responsibility.

○ Being ill: as a way of avoiding core issues and retreating from the world.

○ Any form of attention-seeking, diversionary behaviour.

Remember that avoidance strategies are just that, and will merely take you further away from a solution and feed your fears by avoiding the issues and burying them. Instead of acknowledging that you can take responsibility for the situation and your feelings about it, what you are really saying is, 'I'm going to escape; I can't cope.'

Attitude and personality

The greater your willingness to take responsibility for your own emotions and behaviour – rather than blaming the situation on others or thinking it is unfair – the greater your resilience to stress. Wayne Froggatt calls it being 'inner-controlled' with the ability to:

○ Get on with life now, rather than dwelling on the past.

○ Take setbacks in your stride.

○ Believe in self-determination rather than luck.

○ Take a problem-solving approach.

○ Be flexible and open-minded in considering solutions.

○ Be assertive rather than passive or aggressive when relating to other people.
○ Take responsibility, but don't fall into a trap of self-blame.

Case study: One door shuts and another opens

Ahmed was a sales representative in telecommunications who was made redundant. He was 56 and he was devastated; with only nine years to go until his retirement, he was angry, disappointed, scared and shaken. His self-confidence had taken a real blow.

Ahmed's worries about his mortgage and other financial commitments brought on insomnia, headaches and stomach upsets but, being a true salesman, he had an innately positive outlook. Within a fortnight (after talking things through with his wife) he had turned his attitude around: his redundancy package would give him three months' leeway, so he didn't need to panic. Ahmed had excellent contacts in the industry and sound business sense, so he decided to explore the possibilities of starting his own consultancy. He also considered downshifting for a while in order to release capital on his home that would allow himself and his wife to go travelling for a year. Suddenly the world offered a wealth of opportunities.

The length of time the pressure has continued for

The longer the pressure has existed, the harder it is to remain resilient to stress. Tiredness, exhaustion, grief, erosion of confidence and physical weakness all play their part in whittling away tenacity and commitment.

In order to combat stress you need to arm yourself with the right practical and psychological tools:

❍ Self-direction: The ability to set short-, mid- and long-term goals, making sure they are working to your own – and not someone else's – agenda.

❍ Commitment: To pursuing your goals rather than dreaming about them.

❍ Decision-making: Draw on the views of others, but make your *own* decisions.

❍ The ability to resist blaming others: Instead, identify causes and find useful solutions.

❍ Recognition that managing stress is a skill like any other, and that by careful planning and focus it is possible to combat it.

❍ Awareness that the symptoms of stress need treating and that there is no shame in getting medical advice or help.

The more flexible you can be in your attitude to the causes and effects of your stress, the more likely it is that you will be able to find positive and creative solutions to your situation. It may be difficult, but it is helpful to think of your situation as a new challenge rather than a personal threat. This thinking will reinforce the understanding that, no matter how desperate a situation might seem, you *can* change direction.

Let's get physical

The 'fight or flight' response is a short-term survival technique that originally evolved to encourage us to move physically either towards, or away from, a threat. In modern times our stress is more likely to be caused by excessive mental rather than physical pressure, and as a result this means that the body's physical 'fight or flight' impulse is not used effectively. If the adrenaline-charged, hormonal response is not channelled into physical energy, we become increasingly tense, pent-up and anxious. If the threat continues for an extended period of time, the body will continue to produce yet more adrenaline and cortisol. As this process goes on unabated, the rise in hormone level continues to increase rather than decrease our levels of stress.

So the answer is simple: get your body moving. Our bodies were built to be active, but these days most people spend far too many hours each day, each week, each year in a static position, tense and huddled over a computer or in front of the television set.

If you enjoy exercise and have a history of being involved in sport, you probably won't need too much encouragement to take it up again...once you have scheduled a firm time slot in your diary. Those who have less happy memories of sport or the gym, and those who are over 40 or fairly unfit, will need to take things a little more slowly. (If, on the other hand, you *are* in shape and exercise regularly but you are still suffering from nervous tension, you probably need to slow down rather than speed up.)

If you need more incentive to get back into shape, remember that, as well as increasing tension, a lack of exercise causes the body to age prematurely: wrinkles in the skin appear faster, hair gets thinner, muscles lose their tone, and the body lays down fat more easily. In addition, if you don't use your muscles and lungs to their optimum capacity on a regular basis you will become increasingly weak, feeble and fatigued – whatever your age.

Case study: 'Use it or lose it'

Kate was a freelance journalist who juggled deadlines with her other job as a mother. Lucky to have a fast metabolism and always on the go, she had never had a weight problem but she lived in a constant state of tension because of the demands of work and home. She ate well, but regularly gave in to chocolate cravings and drank more than the recommended number of units of alcohol per week. In her 20s and 30s she had had few health problems, but as she entered her early 40s, work pressures meant that she now spent long hours seated at her desk and her weight had increased by 12 kilos. It was a real shock when she started to develop respiratory problems.

Her GP told her that her lifestyle was putting her body under undue stress and prescribed an inhaler. Alarmed, she began to see herself as weak, middle-aged and unfit. Medically, the incident was minor, but for Kate it was a real wake-up call. She needed to get her body moving and her life back in balance in order to regain her energy levels and self-respect – as well as her health. In conversation with her GP Kate realized that her beliefs about herself were out of kilter with reality. Her usual response to stress and pressure was no longer appropriate and she had to change for her own good and for that of her family.

Usual response

○ *I can cope with whatever is thrown at me.*

○ *If I move fast enough I will get there in time.*

○ *I can't go out until the task is finished.*

○ *I'll work through the night if necessary.*

○ *I've spent all day on this and I still haven't finished it.*

○ *I can't say 'no' to work – I've got a child to feed.*

○ *I will start to get fit...when I've finished this project.*

With the help of her GP, Kate began to accept her age and stage in life and was able to create a new reality – as well as putting together a realistic action plan for positive change:

Altered reality

○ *I thought I was coping, but I'm not.*

○ *I've neglected myself and have put on too much weight.*

○ *I'm getting older and I need to nurture my body in order to keep it healthy.*

○ *My body is showing signs of chronic stress and it scares me.*

○ *I owe it to my son to take better care of my health.*

○ *I find it difficult to maintain a balance, so I need help to achieve change.*

○ *There's no reason why I can't change – other people do.*

Action plan for dealing with her stress

Her action plan seems straightforward and easy on paper, but Kate knew she would find it a real challenge to change her ways permanently and consistently. This being so, her GP encouraged her to come back in three months' time so they could review her progress together.

Immediate action

○ Throw out chocolate, coffee and any form of instant, processed or junk food.

○ Reduce the strain of chores and order fresh fruit and vegetables (and all other grocery shopping) online for ease.

○ Draw up a realistic, task-driven schedule – which should include regular breaks.

○ Establish a routine of no more than nine hours of work a day and at least eight hours' sleep a night.

○ Make one night a week a sacrosanct time for socializing.

○ Start or end each day with a 20-minute walk.

Long-term plan

○ Join a gym within the next month – and ask for advice from gym staff/trainers.

○ Schedule two short holidays per year.

○ Take up a sport or physical activity within two months.

○ Set monthly targets to measure gym attendance and progress in order to keep up the momentum.

○ Keep a simple daily journal to log progress and pitfalls.

Kate's action plan might seem quite ambitious for someone who has been sedentary and physically unmotivated for so long, but the keys to her success are her willingness to plan and set targets, her decision to involve an advisor, and her idea to keep a journal. It is only as a result of steady progress and careful routine that long-term changes will occur.

What's your reaction to stress?

The effects of stress can be very isolating, but that doesn't mean that you are the only person being affected by stress. Your attitude and the way in which you deal with your situation can affect other people around you. Are you one of the people who make a stressful situation worse? Or are you a trouble-shooter? Or perhaps you are someone who causes stress in the first place?

Stephen Williams and Susan Iacovou are human resource specialists with many years' experience of organizational change and stress management in business. In *The Pressure's On* they identify three main 'stress reaction types':

Stress transmitters

People who are obviously under stress and unable to cope, those who think they are coping but are not, and those who don't want to take responsibility for their personal feelings of pressure, are 'stress transmitters': in other words, they pass their stress on to somebody else. These people may be so used to operating in adrenaline-fuelled extremes that stress has become a habit. Their inappropriate behaviours can cause a stress reaction in others who then become tense, anxious or irritable.

Included in this group are:
○ Perfectionists
○ Procrastinators
○ Crisis managers

Stress transmitters are often unaware of the negative impact they are having on others and may cause much of the stress they want to avoid. (If you think this is you, see p. 76 for strategies for effective planning and change.)

Stress dumpers

These are the people who become stressed and who then get rid of these unwanted pressures by 'dumping' their stress onto someone else – leaving that person to pick up the pieces and heighten their own stress levels as a result.

Included in this group are:

○ Those who are over-emotional
○ Those who are aggressive or bullying
○ Quitters
○ Ineffective delegators.

Members of this group are the least likely to suffer from stress themselves because of their unique ability to pass it on to others. It can be difficult to spot whether you fall into this category, so ask those closest to you for their opinion. (If you think that you share some of these traits when under pressure, see p. 106 for ways to communicate more effectively.)

Stress carriers

The carriers are the people who take the stress on board and get on with it as best they can.

Included in this group are:

○ Problem-solvers
○ Leaders

o Managers
o Carers
o 'Rescuers'.

People in this group tend to have a healthy response to stress initially, but need to be aware that if the source of stress continues unabated there may be repercussions further down the line. Those who have a tendency to 'suffer in silence' may be carrying undue levels of stress, despite their apparent ability to cope. Stress carriers need to learn to communicate their needs in a calm and assertive way. (See p. 106 for guidance on communication.)

What is your stress-reaction type?

In the face of pressure we may collapse, freeze, blame others, run away or adopt a coping strategy. If you know and understand your stress reaction type you will be more conscious of the ways in which you could respond more appropriately, as well as most effectively.

Step 1

Put aside ten minutes to identify three situations in the last six months in which you have found yourself suffering from stress. These can have occurred at home or at work, but they should all illustrate what happens to you when you are subject to an unmanageable level of pressure.

Step 2

Take ten minutes to look at each situation individually and record in the following grid what you did (the action you took); how you behaved (whether calmly, irrationally, and so on), and how you felt at the time (for example, fearful, panicky, angry, put upon).

Step 3

Consider the three stress reaction types described on pp. 55–7. Does your behaviour fit with one or more of the categories? Do you exhibit the same traits in situations at home as at work, or does it depend on the circumstances?

Step 4

Arrange time to discuss your conclusions with someone you trust can give you an objective opinion. Do they share your view? What is their experience of you when you are in a stressed state? How does your response affect others and their relationship with or response to you?

Step 5

Consider ways in which you might have handled things

	SITUATION 1
WHAT I DID	
HOW I BEHAVED	
HOW I FELT	
WHAT OTHERS FEEL ABOUT MY BEHAVIOUR	

(Adapted from *The Pressure's On,* p. 59. BBC.)

more effectively and refer to Chapter 4 to plan how to
manage your responses more calmly in future.

Case study: The stress carrier

*Meg had had been married to her husband for 25 years and
together they had three teenage boys and an eight year-old
daughter. The couple were badly in debt and Meg was holding
down two part-time jobs in addition to running the home. She
was perpetually exhausted and constantly behind with the
domestic chores. To cap it all, their youngest child was under-
performing at school. The children were used to seeing Meg
in a state of stress and so were unsympathetic to her plight.
Her husband was away from home a lot so she had to cope on
her own most of the time – and the strain of responsibility and
exhaustion was beginning to tell on Meg.*

*One evening, Meg broke down in tears as she talked to a
friend about her situation. When she looked up she saw that
her daughter had got out of bed and was standing at the door*

SITUATION 2	SITUATION 3

looking worried. Instead of empathizing with her anxiety, Meg felt something snap inside herself. She screamed uncontrollably at the alarmed child to get back to her room and to stop eavesdropping.

In that moment her child was forced to bear the full brunt of Meg's stress – and distress, and it was then that Meg began to wonder whether it was the level of stress in the house that was affecting her daughter's performance at school.

The next day, Meg took time to apologize to her daughter and explain that it was not her fault that mummy was upset. They agreed a special 'us' time to do homework and relax for half an hour each evening from then on.

Whatever level of pressure you are under, and however stressed you might be feeling, the situation *will* change. Whether it changes for the better or for the worse depends partly upon external factors but, crucially, it also depends on your personal attitude and how you choose to respond and plan for what is happening to you and around you. Allowing things to drift until outside circumstances force change is never to be recommended.

Time management

When you're under pressure, the one thing you never have enough of is time. As priorities begin to battle for your attention, or you feel as if your life is no longer your own, it can be very hard to stand back, look hard at the reality of the situation and reassume control. But regaining control is absolutely what you need to do; and the less time you have, the more important it is for you to get ahead of the game in order to avoid becoming a victim of circumstance.

Most of us know the basic principles of time management. It sounds so straightforward – and it is!

○ Plan ahead
○ Make lists
○ Prioritize
○ Decide on start dates, or times, and end dates, or times, for specific tasks.
○ Delegate – at home as well as at work.
○ Review progress and follow up rigorously.
○ Repeat, on an ongoing basis.

Ahhh – if only life were that simple! Instead, at the very moment when we are under the most pressure – to meet a deadline, to make a difficult phonecall, to make a doctor's appointment – we apply diversionary tactics. Suddenly the vacuuming needs to be done, it's crucial to send an email to someone who hasn't been in touch for years, you have to nip out to the post office...You get the idea.

Procrastination is known as 'the thief of time' for good reason, and this villain rears its head no matter how often we rewrite our 'to-do' lists, or despair when someone makes last-minute demands on our time.

Why, when the last thing we want is more stress, do we insist on bringing it upon ourselves? In order to understand that we are personally responsible for many of our own difficulties, we need to look at our behaviours. There are common characteristics amongst 'time thieves', some of which might sound rather familiar...

You *can* develop self-discipline

It can be hard to face up to the fact that you need to be tougher on yourself to gain control of your life. At times when you are under increased pressure from other people it is even more important to keep a tight rein on your own priorities in order to free yourself from negative stress and create time to enjoy the more relaxing things in life. If you don't, there is a possibility that your stressed-out behaviour will remain a habit long after the pressure has subsided, which may have disastrous implications for relationships at home, at work or with friends.

Ask yourself: 'Is this me?'

○ I never, or rarely, make lists.
○ I rarely set personal goals or deadlines.
○ I often miss deadlines set by others.
○ I am easily distracted by unimportant tasks.
○ I have a low level of concentration.
○ I have a scattergun approach to completing tasks.
○ I am always ready to get involved in discussions.
○ I always treat social calls as top priority.

You *can* say no

Being helpful to others is a very clever method of procrastinating, because you can say that you had no choice but to help. But, of course, you *did* have a choice. There are very few requests that cannot be deferred, delayed or declined if you have a more pressing priority.

Low self-esteem, an inability to be assertive or, in contrast, a sense of self-importance, are often at the root of the need to say 'yes', unquestioningly, to the needs of others. There is nothing wrong with helping people, but if you say yes to a request when you really want to say no, you will add significantly to your stress levels and you will also be increasingly time-starving yourself.

Ask yourself: 'Is this me?'

○ I like to be of help and support to others.

○ My self-esteem is based on the regard of others.

○ I don't like to upset or disappoint people.

○ I am driven by a sense of personal duty.

○ I find saying yes is easier than saying no.

○ Self-denial is a long-standing habit.

○ I usually put the demands of others ahead of my own priorities.

○ I am constantly interrupted by other people.

○ I have a tendency to agree to unrealistic deadlines.

○ I find it hard to get rid of callers or visitors quickly.

○ I will usually drop my current task to deal with (non-urgent) enquiries or needs of others.

You don't have to get bogged down

Being overworked is a common cause of stress – and the more stressed you are, the more tired you feel; the more tired you feel, the slower your responses and the lower your productivity. Before long, you feel completely bogged down with nowhere to turn. However, we can all work more effectively and, as a leading manager of the publishing company IPC once remarked, 'If we each worked in a way that saved 10 per cent of our time every day we would gain one month extra a year.'

Ask yourself: 'Is this me?'

○ I find it difficult to delegate or ask others to help.

○ I need to be involved or in control of everything.

○ I am overwhelmed by paper and/or emails.

○ I don't have an effective administration system.

○ I have a tendency to be forgetful.

○ I have poor organizational skills.

○ I probably spend too much time focusing on unimportant details.

○ I take time to write letters, reports or emails because I want to get them right.

○ I am a perfectionist.

Forward planning and project management: the key to living stress-free

Forward-planning and project-management skills apply just as much at home as at work. Think about the last time you briefed a builder to undertake a task and found the result wasn't what you expected; or when you thought you had agreed with your teenage son that he would clean his room – only to find that his interpretation of 'when' was different from yours!

Developing clear focus and the ability to plan ahead are key skills in learning to take control of potential stress factors.

Ask yourself: 'Is this me?'

○ I don't set a timescale for tasks.

○ I tend not to make lists of action points.

○ I don't have clear objectives.

○ I waste time asking the advice of inappropriate people.

○ I have a tendency to stray off the subject.

○ I am not able to get my point of view across clearly.

○ I feel as if people don't listen to me.

○ I find it hard to reach conclusions or agree actions with others.

○ I am not comfortable leading discussions.

○ I tend to see the problems in a situation.

Create a system for tracking information

Being unable to put your hand on a crucial piece of paper, or to know what those living or working close to you have planned over the week ahead, can cause irritating delays and problems that can trigger a major panic attack in someone who is already in a high-stress state.

Ask yourself: 'Is this me?'

○ I live in an untidy environment.

○ I am often forgetful.

○ I tend not to get messages, or forget to pass them on.

○ My paperwork is not filed systematically.

○ I am not usually aware of the priorities of others.

○ I don't know who does what at work.

○ I am always looking for things.

○ I am never sure what to do first.

Develop your communication skills

Communicating our needs to others in a clear and effective way and then following through in an appropriate manner is a critical skill in managing pressure and avoiding stress. We all communicate, but the problem is that other people don't always understand what we want or what we are saying. Four people listening to the same person making one request will each interpret it slightly differently, and the only person who really understands what is required is the person who made the request in the first place.

Ask yourself: 'Is this me?'

○ I tend to think about things in depth only after the event.

○ I feel isolated and alone with my problems.

○ I don't believe anyone else will understand.

○ I never get a clear answer to my requests or questions.

○ I find it hard to recognize that other people's priorities may be different from mine.

○ I usually wait for someone else (or an organization) to make the first move.

○ I don't like to ask other people in case it's inconvenient.

○ If I mention something once, I expect others to act or remember without reminder.

○ I haven't got time to communicate in more depth.

○ I tend to assume that others will understand my motives.

Change your self-talk

One of the key ways in which we can turn our situation around from a high-stress state to manageable pressure is through self-talk. Tony Buzan in *Embracing Change* and *Use Your Head* calls this 'Meta-Positive Thinking'. The idea behind this is that your brain believes only what it is told. If, therefore, you tell yourself that it is going to be a terrible day, the chances are that it will be! If, on the other hand, you tell yourself that you have the ability to manage the challenges that you face, your brain will understand, and you will succeed.

Managing stress is the process of making sure that the problem is not allowed to become larger than it really is.

Case study: *Managing problems and time*

Jasmine is a single parent with a delightful three-year-old daughter, Abi, who has Down's syndrome. Jasmine is half-way through her training as a special-needs teacher, which she hopes will give her the flexibility to spend time with Abi as well as bring in a professional income. Abi's father has recently got back in touch and now wants access. This is a problem for Jasmine on an emotional level and she spends several days in personal torment – jeopardizing her exam revision – as she revisits past hurts. Eventually, Jasmine comes to the conclusion that her response is inappropriate and that contact with her father is necessary for Abi.

Knowing that she can't allocate time to deal with the situation at the moment, Jasmine decides to simplify matters. So she writes to Abi's father explaining that she values the contact on Abi's behalf but will be unable to follow up at the moment as she has other commitments. She promises to contact him again on a specific date in eight weeks' time and makes a note in her diary to contact a family mediator to gain personal and objective support in the meantime.

In this way, Jasmine acknowledges the seriousness of the situation, but she does not allow it to control her at a time when her personal long-term objectives are the priority.

Another strategy is to put your situation into perspective by imagining a scenario much worse than your own. It is no surprise that those who have suffered painful bereavement or other loss often find themselves drawn towards doing voluntary work for support organizations. The act of giving time and attention to others who are suffering enables them to put their own experiences into some form of general perspective. This is not a 'cure' for grief or depression, however, and if symptoms are persistent it is important to seek more professional advice as well.

How you can help yourself – step 3: Your stress, your choice

Be aware

We cannot always choose the situation we find ourselves in, but there is always scope to choose our approach and attitude to dealing with the stress that may follow.

❍ What's your stress-reaction type? Do you cope calmly, or do you flap? Are you a stress transmitter? A stress dumper? Or a stress carrier? Take some time to assess how you behave when under stress, how you feel, how your response affects others, and how you might change your response in future.

❍ Be tolerant of yourself and get professional help if the levels of pressure have been continuing for an unreasonable length of time.

❍ Be honest with yourself about negative habits that might be adding to your pressure, such as your approach to time management, delegation, planning and paperwork.

❍ Be aware of signs of stress symptoms in others, so that you are able to respond to them in a way that acknowledges that they are under pressure. It is more likely to diffuse the situation.

Take action

○ Decide what you want to change in your current situation, rather than waiting to 'see what happens' or leaving things to chance. Taking a problem-solving approach will give you an immediate sense of control.
○ Resolve to look forwards instead of backwards, and to believe in yourself rather than fate or luck.
○ Focus on your use of time; decide whether changing the way you organize your life could reduce your stress levels.

Commit to change

○ Permanent change is about changing a mind-set, which means not only changing attitude, but also putting ideas into action. To prove to yourself that you are committed to beating stress, set yourself time-bound, written goals, so that you can see yourself change over time.
○ If you are unfit, commit to just 20 minutes a day to start walking, dancing, running – whatever motivates you to build a new fitness habit. It is a fast and healthy way to strengthen your body as well as your inner resolve. Write it in the diary, on the fridge, on the hall mirror: anywhere that means you can't possibly avoid or forget the reminder.
○ If you are someone who finds it hard to relax, try swapping some of your fitness time for a music event, a yoga class, a reiki session or a visit to see a friend whom you can rely on to see the lighter side of life.
○ If any of the time-stealing tendencies on pp. 62–6 apply to you, use positive self-talk techniques to turn your attitude round. There are more guidelines about how to achieve this in Chapter 4.

Shape up for stress

Strategies to improve health and well-being

The preceding chapter looked at stress-inducing behaviours, so this chapter will now offer you practical suggestions and strategies to keep these at bay and to 'shape up' your lifestyle. Improving your physical health and your mental well-being are important steps towards making you start to feel more alive and more in control.

Acceptance

One of the most powerful ways to cope with the negative effects of stress is to accept that it is a part of your life that you need to face head on. Acceptance does not mean giving in or choosing not to change your situation; it means 'starting where you are' with conscious awareness of the pressures you are facing, the impact they are likely to have on your physical, mental and spiritual well-being, and what you need to do to help your body to cope with these pressures.

If you deny that you are feeling pressure, the impact of stress is likely to get worse. Stress uses up the body's resources, so it will affect your health, mood, appetite, libido, mental alertness, productivity, your relationships and your susceptibility to illness and depression. Bearing this in mind, it makes sense to plan to replenish your reserves on all fronts.

Remember that stress does not *have* to be the inevitable result of pressure. This chapter looks at how we can tackle the *sources* of stress, rather than the symptoms. If you are able to change your perception of your situation as well as change self-sabotaging habits, you will be able to avoid stress occurring altogether.

Work-pressure audit

You are under pressure if:

❍ You regularly work more than fifty hours per week.

❍ You take few or no breaks during the day.

❍ You work mainly alone.

❍ You regularly take work home with you.

❍ You have high expectations of yourself.

❍ You have a fear of letting people down.

❍ You find it hard to switch off at the end of the day.

❍ You frequently cancel social arrangements because you have to work.

❍ You rarely take time out to relax.

❍ You regularly drink more than two units of alcohol a night. (A unit is half a pint of beer or one small glass of wine.)

❍ There is a history of heart disease or stroke in the family.

❍ Fruit and vegetables are not a substantial part of your diet.

❍ You regularly eat your main meal later than 9pm.

❍ You can't remember the last time you had a good laugh.

○ You haven't had a week off work (in whatever form) for over a year.

If you are a person who frequently puts yourself under more pressure than necessary, you need to learn how to adapt to stress – and how to avoid it.

Stress-beating resources

Since stress occurs when the pressure we are under increases beyond our capacity to cope, it makes sense both to reduce the degree of pressure exerted on us as well as to increase our resources for coping.

External resources include: friends, relations, educational and professional training, finance, home environment, pets, holidays, sporting activities and other hobbies.

Personal resources include: self-belief, knowledge, attitude, skills, personality, health and fitness.

Self-belief

The most effective stress-beater of all is self-belief: the belief that you can genuinely beat stress and use it for personal growth. By doing so you will release your potential and transform a distressing state into one that is much more manageable.

Self-belief begins in the mind. Experts such as Tony Buzan explain in great detail how the mind works and how the subconscious mind influences and drives the conscious mind.

To bring about personal change you need first to reprogramme your subconscious with positive, self-fulfilling thoughts. A simple and effective way to achieve this is creative visualization techniques. The best way of using this method is to sit in a darkened, quiet room and take time to focus on and regulate your breathing. Visualize the skill, feeling or situation that you want to transform, see yourself in your changed state and take yourself step by step through the transformation.

Case study: Visualization in action

Liam worked as a teacher. He had got into the habit of working late at school every evening and then carrying home a heavy, bulging bag full of books and papers for marking. Already tired out by the time he got home, nine times out of ten he didn't open the bag and had to carry it all the way back to work in the morning. He was wearing himself into the ground, but he seemed unable to leave school without the bag – it was as if it had become a symbol of the weight he was carrying and the stress he was under. A colleague with some experience of hypnotherapy techniques suggested that he try visualizing a different approach, and, with some scepticism, Liam agreed to give it a go.

In a darkened room, Liam sat in a chair with his hands placed loosely in his lap and took several deep breaths to relax and clear his mind. He imagined himself at the end of the working day: tidying his desk, writing a list of priorities for the morning and leaving a pile of papers on the desk and his bag on the floor by the door. He then visualized himself walking down the corridor, out of the school and over to the station – without his bag. Liam continued the visualization through every stage of his journey,

right up the steps to his front door, into his house and until he
saw his hallway with no bag there and no reminder of work for
the evening. He sat quietly, absorbing the feeling of relief and
lightness that it brought, then he opened his eyes.

When the end of the day came, Liam remembered this
visualization and re-enacted this scene. For the first time in two
years he was able to go home and relax, leaving work behind
him. Liam was amazed at the power of such an apparently simple
exercise. However, this was a real turning point for him, and
from that day on he very rarely took work home unless he was
absolutely obliged to do so and, while still working long hours,
he was at least able to make his home a relaxation zone. Spurred
on by this victory, Liam used visualization techniques to help him
achieve other goals, too.

Another way to retrain your mind to overcome stress is
by changing the way you talk to yourself. People under
pressure tend to feed this feeling by telling themselves that
they are useless, badly organized, likely to be found out for
their 'failings', etc. (In Chapter 4 we will explore this idea
further with suggestions on how you can improve your
communication skills and positive self-talk.)

Long-term stress resilience

If your situation is high-pressured, but under control
and would not deteriorate if you adopted a more gradual
strategy for dealing with stress, you might be best trying
a long-term resilience technique. This is a whole-life
approach to stress management and will take into account
your physical, behavioural and social resources. (Other

chapters go into greater depth to explain how each of these resources is a positive tool for changing negative stress into positive pressure.)

Your physical resources
○ Relaxation and breathing
○ Healthy eating
○ Exercise.

Your behavioural resources
○ Time-management skills (and planning)
○ Assertiveness
○ Communication skills.

Your social resources
○ Balancing home and work
○ Building your social-support network.

Short-term coping

If your stress is acute and there is no time in the short term to put in place a lifestyle strategy for dealing with pressure, the emphasis has to be on managing your symptoms of stress and using techniques to calm breathing and change the physical state of the body. This kind of work will directly influence your emotional state of mind and behaviour.

Breathwork, visualization and positive thinking are all valuable coping techniques for dealing with short-term (and long-term) stress. (See p. 20 for a practical breathing exercise to help beat stress.)

Shape up and live

Shaping up your mental and physical well-being are crucial aspects of learning to manage stress and anxiety. The core skills are:

○ Keeping life's pressures in perspective.
○ Prioritizing goals so you know where you are headed.
○ Planning your time to make your life your own.
○ Taking action to beat procrastination.
○ Giving yourself a break.

Life planning and time management are skills like any other; and they need to be practised to get them right. If you find your self-discipline has flagged, and that you have slipped back into old habits, ask yourself why, then get yourself back on track in a conscious manner. You can change and you *will* change – *if* you want to.

Put off putting things off

Since we all have the same number of hours in a day, why is it that some people are able to get everything done on their own terms, within a normal working day, while others use up much of their private time to complete these same tasks? Feeling as if you are behind with your work or will never catch up with everything you have to do causes stress – and once the saturation point has been reached it can be difficult to achieve anything at all.

Be aware of the procrastination traps

○ Poor prioritizing: Doing small jobs to avoid starting the large ones.

○ Perfectionism: Over-researching and gathering data to avoid starting work.

○ Phone calls: Taking calls when you shouldn't, or making them at a time when the recipient won't be there.

○ Delaying tactics: Getting up every five minutes to make a cup of coffee, to speak to someone, to look something up, and so on, merely to avoid completing a task.

Action plan to beat procrastination

○ Have a schedule: Break large projects into manageable portions, then schedule a realistic start date for each task – including a start and stop time for each daily stage.

○ Just do it! Commit yourself to the start time you have set – and start! Keep going until the scheduled stop time. If your times are right, the overall deadline will be met.

○ Progress check: Monitor your progress as you work through the task and it will give you a sense of momentum and achievement.

○ Don't gild the lily: Be clear about when you have finished the task – not everything has to be perfect to be effective. If you are going to meet your deadlines, you need to learn to let go of your work – even if you think a few details might look better changed.

○ Work on one task at a time: Keep focused and don't juggle tasks. If you work in an office, keep any paper on your desk to a minimum. Avoid distractions and the temptation to go off at a tangent.

○ Restrict internet and mobile phone access: It is very easy to get into the habit of checking messages as a boredom reflex, but before you know it you will be drawn into replying to unimportant emails and texts that eat into your valuable allocated time for a task.

○ Be self-disciplined about phone calls: Use voicemail to screen calls when you are busy and make sure you return important calls promptly.

○ Face tough tasks head on: If you have a difficult call to make – make it. *Don't* waste time composing a perfect email instead, and if it's difficult news you have to deliver, do it face-to-face if at all feasible.

○ Prioritize tasks: Create a 'to-do' list. Be clear about which are the most time-sensitive and crucial tasks to be completed. Review and revise the list at the beginning and end of every day – but restrict the number of times a particular task is carried forwards.

○ Make your motto 'Do it now': Overcoming procrastination is a real step towards beating stress and regaining control over the pressures in your life.

ACTION	PRIORITY	START DATE OR TIME

(Adapted from *Managing Time,* pp. 17–18, BBC.)

How to do a 'to-do' list

An effective 'to-do' list is more than just a list and can
be adapted for use at home as well as at work. To become
a genuinely useful management tool it needs to include
time-bound headings. (See the table below.)

The art of prioritizing

Many people, when faced with a list of things they need
to achieve in a day, find it difficult to decide which is truly
the most important. Commercial priorities can be easier to
order than those that are home-orientated, because nine
times out of ten the top priority is revenue-driven (except
in the caring professions). On the other hand, the sheer
volume of time-sensitive work can be hard to manage. In
the home, priorities tend to be a more moveable feast and
are dependent upon other people's needs in the family,
whether you are earning, are supporting other people,

END DATE OR TIME	GIVE TASK TO OR ASK FOR HELP FROM	REVIEW

are in good health, have financial concerns and so on. Emotional requirements have greater importance in the home and the priorities are not always as obvious. It can be useful to take stock of the general priorities in your life and to be aware of how you categorize them. Do you have your priorities 'right' or should something else be in your number-one slot? Everyone's lists will be different.

Business priorities

Revenue-generating	1
Customer relations	2
Personnel management/training	3
Administration	4
Planning and budgeting	5

Personal priorities

A safe home environment	1
Good health (diet, sleep, exercise)	2
Work/income/finance	3
Family commitments	4
Social contact	5

Once you are aware of what your main priorities are it can be easier to juggle tasks on a daily basis. A 'to-do' list becomes a useful tool to combat stress at source if the tasks are also prioritized by level of importance. Categorizing tasks on a simple scale of 'A', 'B' or 'C' can simplify your decision-making and help you to pre-plan what to let go of if something unexpected happens.

A: High priority

Tasks that have monetary value and those that have to be completed on time. High-value work is almost always top priority in the workplace.

B: Medium priority

Work that is equally important but has a longer deadline. Today's medium-priority work can become next week's or next month's high priority. Often tasks in this bracket lose out to As and Cs, so it is very important not to forget these medium-priority tasks – and to prioritize separately any preparatory work that needs to be done to complete them.

C: Low priority

Work that can generally be delayed, deferred or delegated or that will not have immediate ramifications. Many people take refuge in low-priority tasks to avoid beginning a high-priority task, as they are often quick or easy to do and give an illusion of progress. If you are regularly spending 60 per cent of your time on administrative and 'non-productive' tasks, you need to review how you are using your time.

Case study: Transforming old habits

Maria is an interior designer and a mother who is forever over-committing and rushing to get too much done in a day. She has an ongoing 'to-do' list that she adds to as and when things crop up, but she doesn't put start or end times next to the tasks and often finds that an unexpected phone can change the shape of her whole day. She is highly committed to expanding her business, but is forever finding that domestic issues have to take priority.

Maria's reorganized to-do list *(see p. 84)*

(see p. 84)

○ *Prepare special meal for daughter's birthday.*
○ *Vacuum and tidy house ready for birthday meal.*
○ *Complete spec for new retail client X.*
○ *Dental appointment at 2.30pm.*
○ *Chase up invoices.*

Maria's priorities, revised using High (A), Medium (B)

Priority	Task
Work	
A	Complete spec for new retail client X
A	Put portfolio together for meeting tomorrow am
B	Emergency call from favourite client
B	Prepare design spec for private client Y
B	Chase up invoices
C	Research new suppliers
Home	
A	Pick up mother from hairdresser at 12pm
A	Prepare special meal for daughter's birthday
B	Dental appointment at 2.30pm
B	Take daughter shopping
C	Vacuuming and tidying

- ○ *Complete design spec for private client Y.*
- ○ *Pick up mother from hairdresser at 12pm.*
- ○ *Put together portfolio for meeting tomorrow morning.*
- ○ *Research more creative suppliers.*
- ○ *Take daughter late-night shopping.*

---

ow (C) scheme and separated into work and home

Action

The priority. It's new business. First impressions count.

This needs to be done today because it takes time to do well.

After explaining to client that the work can be done in two days' time, but not today, it transpires that he is about to go on holiday, so it isn't needed for a fortnight. Emergency over.

Start at the end of the day if time. Schedule to complete tomorrow.

Schedule for 20 minutes daily to avoid turning into an 'A'.

Time-consuming – reschedule for next week.

Arrange for sister-in-law to collect her instead.

Take her out for a special meal instead. More relaxing for both.

Reschedule (once only) as it is a check-up.

Agree to take her at the weekend – and her friends too.

Can wait until the weekend.

*When a favourite client phones to ask her to do a 'quick' revamp
of the colour scheme that she has delivered earlier in the week,
Maria, with no clear, time-bound goals in place for her other
commitments, finds herself agreeing to fit it in. She feels stressed
already and the day has not yet begun. She decides to make a
cup of coffee and research a few new suppliers on the internet
before getting started – to get the creative ideas flowing. An hour
later she is still online and no further forward with her client's
work.*

*The emergency call from a favourite client has been slotted
in ahead of all her other commitments and has taken her into
panic mode...but what were the real priorities? The reorganized
list on pp. 82–3 shows that once the tasks are prioritized and
time-bound they become manageable and the true priorities
become clearer. It is the difference between being proactive and
planning the day ahead, rather than being reactive and fatalistic
about the consequences.*

Stress-related behaviour

When people are under a great deal of pressure they
display traits that are out of character, that they may not
know they had and may not like. They may even find their
'new' mood hard to handle. For example, a normally calm
and pleasant person may become tense, withdrawn and
defensive, whereas an extrovert and decisive individual
may become demanding and rude. A shy or unassertive
character may break down in tears, while someone more
tough-talking and jovial might lose their temper. Signs of
tension anywhere in a work or a family group will have a

direct impact on everyone else – either directly through mood and attitude, or indirectly through mistakes, accidents, health problems or arguments.

Managing your own behaviour

Think about your own response to stress:

❍ Do you know when you have reached your maximum stress point?

❍ How would others describe your reactions? (Ask your children, if you have them!)

❍ How would you describe your response?

❍ How do you feel when you are stressed?

❍ How does your behaviour change?

The most immediate ways to manage a stress response are to take deep breaths and, if possible, put some distance between you and the source of stress. Using your breath has the benefit of sending more oxygen to the brain, while also calming your heart rate. Creating physical distance will allow you to gain some perspective on the situation and to calm the extremes of emotion. If you are feeling tearful, stand up so that you breathe from the diaphragm and up through the chest.

If you know that you are likely to lose your temper or lash out, train yourself mentally to reprogramme your thinking by having a favourite song that you hum to yourself, a happy or amusing image that you can summon up to change your mood, or simply to state, 'This has made me feel quite angry/upset – I'd like to take a few minutes for myself and then return to discuss it more calmly.'

Case study: Being aware of your stress

Gina knows that when she's under stress she loses her temper and shouts at the children. She's concerned about this because she has noticed that her daughter now does the same thing. She has recently started to make a conscious effort to warn her children in advance when she is very tired, explaining to them that she has had a long and challenging day and may be short-tempered this evening. She has also told them that she will be asking for their help with the household chores – in exchange for small treats.

Influencing others' behaviour

Think about those people closest to you and how you would describe their response to stress.

○ How do you respond to them when they are acting this way?

○ Do you adopt a supportive role, is there a destructive clash or do you remain uninvolved and neutral?

If you are with someone who is in an acute state of stress, take time to let them know that you understand their situation and encourage them to talk. Go for a brief walk with them, breathe deeply, smile or laugh to relieve the tension. Empathize and ask them how they are thinking or feeling. Say what you think or feel and, if possible, put the situation into a broader perspective. Ask for their response and see what they want to do next.

How to change stress-related behaviour

One of the greatest causes of stress is having too much to do on too little sleep. If financial worries are also a factor, stress levels will be high. The following sections offer some further practical strategies for managing stress.

'Smile and the world smiles with you'

There is no doubt that the words of this traditional saying are absolutely right. If you smile at someone they will almost certainly smile back: it is a positive power exchange. At that moment, both people feel appreciated and feel better about life, and thoughts of stress and pressure momentarily disappear. Each of those people is then more likely to smile at someone else that day, and so other people's pressure will also reduce for a moment and the positive benefit of one act multiplies.

Laughter is a powerful force that has been used to release tension ever since travelling minstrels, plays and theatres first used it on stage in both tragedies and comedies. Once you have found a way to laugh at the thing that holds you in its stressful grip, you have taken back your power. Laughter really is the best medicine; it changes mood and facilitates some forms of the healing process. Even in the midst of the horrors of World War I, soldiers in the trenches at the battlefield front found ways to laugh and joke about their leaders. By doing so, a sense of humour unified those who were facing danger and hardship and made life more bearable.

If it's been a while since you had a good laugh, get together with some friends, go to the cinema, watch a TV comedy, video or DVD, or tune into a humorous radio programme. Whatever difficulties you are currently facing, they will be alleviated if you remember to laugh at life.

Create a calm environment

When in a state of stress we tend to create more stress. Have you ever noticed that when you are under pressure your home seems to turn into a sea of chaos overnight? At the very moment you need a calm, safe haven, you find that it has become a symbol of everything that is wrong in your life. If you can restore a sense of calm in at least one room in your home, you will have a place of personal retreat and will have a greater chance of changing your state of mind:

❍ In your kitchen, keep a shopping list of healthy foods so that there is no chance of running out of essentials and reverting to unhealthy snacking. Get rid of unnecessary clutter and any out-of-date goods.

❍ No matter how tight your budget, treat yourself to some lavender oil so you can add a few drops to a relaxing bath at the end of a tiring day. Bath by candlelight, or add some bubbles to the water, and take time to unwind.

❍ Try to prevent your bedroom being used as a dumping ground or a work area, and keep it as a private place to unwind in. Keep fresh flowers in the room – they will lift your spirits with their bright, positive colours.

❍ At the end of a long day, a good meal is something to look forward to, but there is often temptation to eat on the run, in front of the television, or while reading or writing. If you eat at a relaxed pace and focus wholly on the taste and the flavours of your food, you will be less likely to overeat and will enjoy your meal more.

❍ Make a conscious effort not to raise your voice when those around you are driving you crazy. If you can stay

calm in a stressed atmosphere, you will encourage others to
calm down as well.

Simple mood changers

The stress response is habit-forming: the more tense we
become, the less mobile we are and there is a tendency to
retreat inwards and feel set apart from others, and often
to become isolated. But this response can be combated by
adopting other, more healthy, habits:

○ Get some exercise – even if it's only walking around the
block for 20 minutes a day.

○ Pick up the phone and speak to a friend.

○ Listen to some music. Jump up and down or dance
around the room – anything to release the tension.

○ Get a proper night's sleep. Sleep deprivation does not just
lead to exhaustion; it is also harmful to the body. During
sleep the muscles relax, body temperature falls, there is a
reduction in oxygen consumption and our metabolic rate
declines. Our levels of consciousness also sink and the
body has a chance to recharge its batteries.

Avoid avoidance strategies

When under pressure the majority of people will reach
for a diversion or a comfort in order to build artificial
respite from the source of the stress and to numb the
sense of anxiety or fear. But 'self-medication' in the form
of increased use of sleeping pills or alcohol, binge-eating,
smoking cigarettes or cannabis, or other drug use, is always
counter-productive. Don't wait for the situation to get out
of hand before you try different support strategies.

❍ Have a medical check-up. Tell your doctor about your stress symptoms.

Stress and your health

Nutrition plays a very important part in keeping your body healthy during stressful times. Stress symptoms and poor eating habits often go hand in hand. It is especially important that time-starved people make themselves take a break for a healthy lunch and plan ahead to buy food and ingredients that will nurture body and mind, rather than feed their stress problem. As explained in Chapter 1, the increased production of stress hormones diverts core vitamins and minerals away from tissue repair to deal with the body's state of emergency.

We may not always be able to avoid stress, but we can nurture our own health. Establishing a good state of nutritional health should be a top priority in your personal quest to beat stress and reach your own maximum potential.

How stressed is your diet?

Are you eating a high-stress diet? Consider the following questions:

❍ Do you wake up feeling tired?
❍ Do you rely on caffeine to kick-start your day?
❍ Do you drink less than one litre of water a day?
❍ Do you suffer from cravings for sweet foods or chocolate?
❍ Do you tend to feel drowsy after meals?

o Do you suffer from headaches, feel light-headed or become short-tempered if you miss a meal or eat at erratic times?
o Do you sometimes suffer from anxiety for no reason?
o Do you have difficulty making decisions?
o Do you cry easily?
o Are you overweight?

We all know which foods feed stress and what vices we crave under pressure; they are the same ones that provide false, short-term comfort and long-term guilt and health problems: chocolate, alcohol, coffee, cakes, biscuits, fried foods (including chips, burgers and other takeaways), cigarettes, and high-fat savouries such as crisps, salted peanuts and pub snacks. What is not always obvious, however, is what can be eaten instead.

Giving up low-nutrition foods does not mean abandoning all snacks and food comforts, but buying foods that that will help your body and brain to perform more effectively instead. The good news is that the body likes to be healthy, and given half a chance it will revert to full health and quickly reject the nutrition-poor foods that can become a crutch and a craving.

Foods that are 'in'

Eating a balanced diet is both an essential way to keep the effects of stress at bay and a must for strengthening the body's defences in challenging times. There should be no need to eat *more* food during times of increased pressure, but it is important that you choose to eat the *right* foods.

Eat more fruit and vegetables

Eat at least five portions of fruit and vegetables a day, and in times of high stress aim to eat at least eight portions. A single portion is not very large: just an apple, 85g of vegetables or a satsuma. If you swap salty or sugary snacks for easy-to-eat fruit you will exceed your minimum target in no time.

Swap fatty meats for lean meat or oily fish

Saturated fat in food increases the levels of fat in the arteries and puts increased pressure on the heart. Saturated fat also increases cholesterol levels, which may contribute towards heart disease. So it makes sense to eat oily fish, such as mackerel, which are an excellent source of the essential fatty acid (EFA) Omega 3 – important for brain function, coordination and balancing moods, as well as for regulating cholesterol levels.

Eat more pulses and grains

These complex carbohydrates are a good source of fibre and B vitamins and help to maintain constant energy levels during the day. Eating fibre is also helpful in ridding the body of excess fat.

Eat breakfast

You've heard it before, but it's true – eating a breakfast of complex carbohydrates and protein restores blood sugar levels and regulates your energy levels. Eating your main meal in the middle of the day is less stressful for the body, too.

Drink plenty of water

Drink a minimum of eight glasses of water a day: or, if that sounds daunting, try hot water with lemon or fruit or herb teas. Water is vital for good health, and not just when we feel thirsty. The human body is made up of 90 per cent water – it detoxifies the body, nourishes the vital organs and is a critical factor in maintaining energy levels.

Vitamins and minerals

When we're under pressure, the body uses up reserves of vitamins, minerals and essential fatty acids more quickly. While these are readily available in supplement form, it is useful to adjust your diet to accommodate natural sources too. Essential trace minerals include iron, calcium and zinc; the vitamins are A, B, C, D, E and folic acid. The B vitamins in particular (vitamins B1, B2, B3, B6 and B12) are often depleted during times of stress. They are essential for the healthy maintenance of the nervous system and the blood vessels, and can be found in wholegrains, meat, fish, nuts, eggs, pulses, seeds and vegetables.

Avoid low blood sugar (hypoglycaemia)

When blood sugar levels fall too low, the brain becomes less effective and we become tired, anxious, irritable and less able to concentrate. It's then that we are most at risk of reaching for a chocolate bar or a cup of coffee for that instant energy boost. Emotional stress and binge-eating also lead to hypoglycaemia, which in turn leads to fatigue.

To avoid the effects of yo-yoing blood sugar levels, make sure that you eat breakfast and carry fruit or low-fat fruit bars with you throughout the day. Don't miss meals, no matter how much you are tempted to; and pay attention to the GI (glycaemic index) of foods. The idea is to maintain your blood sugar level, rather than allowing it to dip so far that you are drawing on your energy reserves.

Foods that are 'out'

This list is full of the usual suspects, such as saturated fats and refined sugars, but before you hold up your hands in despair, please take a look at some of the alternatives. Foods (and drinks) on this list not only drain the body of energy, they also lower the body's immune defences and use up antioxidants. Once your body gets used to doing without the energy-draining foods, the cravings will diminish and your body will adjust to wanting energy-enhancing foods instead.

Caffeine

If you turn to caffeine to keep awake for long periods of time or because you are used to making a cup of coffee when you feel you need a break from your desk, bear in mind that you are putting strain on your adrenal glands and thus adding to your body's stress. Every time you drink a cup of coffee you raise your pulse rate, which the body reads as anxiety. The brain passes a message to the adrenal glands that it needs to prepare for 'fight or flight' and so the production of stress hormones is increased.

Caffeine is purely a stimulant with no nutritional benefit; it simply depletes the body of B vitamins and raises the pulse rate. Caffeine taken two hours before going to bed will interrupt your sleep pattern. Aim to reduce your caffeine intake, and to replace tea, coffee or cola habits with caffeine-free drinks, such as herb teas, chicory-flavoured granules, diluted fruit juices or mineral water.

If you find it hard to give up caffeine completely, drink a glass of water for every cup of tea, coffee or cola that you have in a day, or try green tea with jasmine, which is lower in caffeine. Bear in mind, too, that there are also high levels of caffeine in chocolate, the herb guarana, and some pain medications.

Stimulants
Caffeine isn't the only stimulant that we turn to in times of stress. Avoid the temptation to try to dull or escape the effects of stress by drinking too much alcohol, smoking tobacco or taking illicit drugs, sedatives or other substances, because in the long run these will exacerbate your condition and make you less able to cope. If you know you have a problem in one or more of these areas, be honest with yourself and seek help. (See Further Resources on p. 179.)

Junk food and snacks
Fast foods and processed foods put stress on the body. If you are prone to eating junk food or chocolate, try carrying healthy snacks with you as an alternative that will keep blood sugar levels constant. Dried apricots, fresh bananas, raisins, nuts and wholegrain bars will help you to avoid the 'sugar-rush' effect of foods high in saturated fats and refined sugars.

If such healthy snacks aren't to your taste, plan to eat good-sized healthy meals at regular times each day so that your body has the energy to take you through to your next meal without the need for snacks.

How you can help yourself – step 4: Shape up your life, your mood and your food
Be aware

Admitting that you're finding it hard to handle pressure can be very difficult, but you may discover that you are showing signs of strain without realizing it. Do you know what kind of impact you have on others when you are under stress? Do you find yourself acting out of character? Even though you may not want to talk, sharing problems and talking about your pressures to those closest to you will help them to understand what you are going through.

Take action

Are you a thinker rather than a doer? Or do you leap in first before planning and prioritizing? If you suspect that you need to plan ahead more effectively than you do at the moment, or know that you have trouble multi-tasking, make use of the guidelines on p. 78.

Start planning ahead and practise allocating start and end times to your daily tasks. This process is just as valuable at home as it is in the workplace. The small amount of time that is taken to plan ahead at the beginning of each day will enable you to spend much more time actually getting things done, rather than having to catch up later in any spare time you end up with. It will also add a sense of momentum to your day.

Commit to change

Planning and prioritizing may seem quite challenging habits to acquire if you're not used to them, but with practice you will learn to allocate each time slot effectively. Bit by bit you will come to understand more about how you work best and how long it takes you to complete tasks during the day – as well as how you spend 'empty' time. If you can commit to making time-bound planning part of your working day it will not only become second nature, but it will also transform your life. In learning to plan ahead you will also see where the true problems lie and will create more time to do other things with your life.

Planning and prioritizing apply equally to your health and to your food. If you de-stress your diet you will de-stress your body and your mind too.

4 Speaking out
Deciding what you want and communicating your needs

'No man, for any considerable period, can wear one face to himself, and another to the multitude, without finally getting bewildered as to which may be true.'

NATHANIEL HAWTHORNE

Be yourself

One of the greatest causes of stress is denial of self. Rejecting who you are, trying to be someone you are not, or constantly making decisions based mainly upon other people's needs and expectations of you, will put you under pressure. The greater the distance between the dutiful you and the real you, and the longer you try to be someone you are not, the more you will become divorced from your true feelings and motivations. This can make it hard for you to express yourself or anticipate how you are going to react and will increase the stress you will experience. Pressure, by its very nature, builds and builds until it reaches a point where it has to blow. Suppression of anger can lead to unexpected or violent outbursts; whereas an inability to express your needs may result in tearful episodes at inappropriate moments.

If you have been putting your own needs to one side for some time – possibly even for years – you might feel disconnected from what motivates you or what you really want. All you know is that you want to be free of the high levels of stress and to get back to being yourself again.

Chapter 1 includes an exercise to help you to decide what you want to change about your situation. The approach can also be used to weigh up what you would like to change about yourself, how you *think* you are perceived, and what you would like to change in the way you communicate with others. The process is especially powerful if used with visualization techniques (p. 73).

Talk it out

A problem shared may not always feel like a problem halved, but it certainly helps to talk about what's on your mind. Problems that exist in isolation have a way of growing out of proportion and to the exclusion of all else.

It is not necessary to discuss directly what is causing you stress to get some comfort from talking to others. How often have you shied away from calling a friend because you felt too low to talk, too tired, or simply not in the mood, only to find when you did call that they have been having problems too? Talking to friends, relatives or listening professionals will help normalize the things that you have on your mind and help you move on. It's likely that you'll find something to laugh about which will change your mood and behaviour and it will remind you to give other people support too.

Passive and aggressive responses to stress

The 'fight or flight' response doesn't just influence the body's chemistry – it also shows in our responses to stress. When tempers flare unexpectedly, physical injuries occur more frequently or tears flow from nowhere, you can be sure that the body has been given a 'fight or flight' message – and it is expressing itself inappropriately.

When we are under pressure, we rarely see how we appear to others. A person who communicates in an unassertive manner may be aware that they are not heard, but they are unlikely to categorize themselves as passive. Likewise, a person who is aggressive in response to a situation is unlikely to realize the overbearing impact they are having on those around them, as they often believe themselves to be the victim of the situation.

In order to regain control over the causes of pressure and the effects of stress, we need to become more self-aware and develop ways of expressing ourselves that are assertive rather than passive or aggressive; ways that show we believe we have choice and power over the situation – rather than being powerless victims of circumstance.

The passive 'flight' response to stress includes characteristics such as:

o Avoiding eye contact.

o Talking in a quiet, strained voice.

o Not finishing sentences.

o Hesitant, faltering speech.

o Face flushing easily.

o Nervous hand movements – for example, fiddling with clothes, rings or other objects.

- Backing away from the other person, physically.
- Apologizing a lot.
- Feeling guilty and taking undue responsibility or blame.
- Agreeing without questioning.

Case study: Tackling passive stress behaviour

Geoff thought of himself as an assertive person and had no trouble communicating or exerting influence in a clear and effective way when he was at home with his family or with his friends – but at work it was different. His voice went unheard in group situations, he was overlooked for senior management roles, and he found it hard to delegate effectively to his team.

The core problems stemmed from Geoff's lack of self-esteem, which showed in his posture and body language (see p. 113), and his increasing guilt that he was falling behind with work. An inability to ask for help and to delegate effectively meant that he felt he was always 'on the back foot' – and he was becoming increasingly apologetic and edgy. It was hard for his team to respect him or for his colleagues to rely on him when he was so obviously stressed. The situation was destroying his self-confidence and he was exhausted by his workload. He was coping with the pressure as best he could, but his passive behaviour was beginning to transmit his stress to others in his team.

Fortunately he was highly regarded by his manager and he was persuaded to attend an assertiveness course. The solutions to Geoff's problems were threefold:

- To change his physical state by learning to relax his breathing, improve his posture and to slow down.
- To change his emotional state by positive self-talk (see p. 66) and self-belief.

○ *To change his behaviour by taking control of his workload through planning, prioritizing and effective delegation.*

The pressure didn't diminish straight away because it took time for him to change his behaviours – but over a period of months his self-esteem grew as he brought about change and began to deliver results.

'Anyone can become angry: that is easy. To be angry with the right person, to the right degree, at the right time, for the right purpose, and in the right way: that is not easy.'
ARISTOTLE

The aggressive 'fight' response to stress includes:
○ Glaring/staring.
○ Speaking in a loud voice.
○ Interrupting a lot.
○ Flushed face.
○ Finger wagging.
○ Posturing – with hands on hips.
○ Moving towards the other person, physically.
○ Blaming others.
○ Stating personal opinions as facts.

An aggressive response is easier to spot than a passive response because it is louder and has more immediate impact on others. Overtly aggressive people are stress transmitters and stress dumpers (see pp. 55–6) who move into 'fight' mode when under pressure.

Case study: The impact of aggressive stress response

Philippa was a self-confident and naturally ebullient character who wouldn't take no for an answer and was used to railroading those around her to get her own way. When things were running smoothly she was good company and fun to be with, but at any sign of pressure she would lose her cool, raise her voice, and blame anyone and everyone for her own dilemma. She made friends and lost them easily. She had made her own way in life and wasn't about to admit to any sign of weakness.

What Philippa rarely showed to those around her was her personal vulnerability and her dread of failure. Too much pain and disappointment at an early age meant she wasn't about to let anyone get too close, and so her aggression stemmed from a fear of showing weakness. She believed that if she gave in to her vulnerability, even once, she would break down completely and never recover herself. Her way of dealing with stress was to party hard and to drink as much as possible to numb her feelings.

Inevitably, her health began to suffer. Fortunately, her boyfriend was not afraid to stand up to her robust nature and he encouraged her to seek help for her drinking. He also suggested she should consider an anger-management or an assertiveness course, to help her to relate to other people in a calmer way.

Passive and aggressive responses are opposite sides of the same coin. Someone who is passive at work may let off steam by becoming aggressive within the safety of their own home. Likewise, someone who is aggressive at work may become passive during conflict at home. The point is, the tension has to express itself somewhere – and that can mean it diverts itself inwards and contributes towards illness.

Look at how you cope when you are under pressure, and work on skills that will help, such as assertiveness, communication and negotiation.

Most of us are capable of being both passive and aggressive on occasion – it depends on the situation. Reflecting on what is your dominant style under stress will help you to gain insight into others' responses towards you:

Ask yourself:

○ When do I tend to react passively?

○ How do I behave? What do other people do?

○ When do I tend to react aggressively?

○ How do I behave? How do others behave?

○ Why do I respond differently in one situation compared with another?

○ What do I think are the triggers that make others respond in these ways?

○ What are the costs to my well-being of reacting in these ways?

Situations that tend to prompt either a passive or an aggressive response include:

○ Being criticized (often repeatedly) – whether justly or unjustly.

○ Being in a situation where you want to say 'no', but you can't.

○ Not being consulted about a decision that concerns you.

○ Wanting to complain, but feeling constrained.

○ When someone disagrees with you.

○ When criticizing someone (and feeling uncomfortable about it).

○ When feeling drained of self-confidence and self-esteem.
○ When feeling under undue pressure or stress.
○ When feeling afraid or under threat.
○ When the other person is showing similar characteristics and is either unduly passive or threatening.

What lies behind these situations and responses is a sense of a loss of control; a feeling that others are dictating the way we should behave, or think. What leads us to believe that another person may have more sway over our behaviour than we do ourselves? It is all in the mind: in the way we speak and think.

Think of the difference in your physical response between being asked to do something and told to do something:

(a) 'Mary and Peter have invited us to a party on Saturday. I've told them that you won't be able to go to because you're playing football.'

(b) 'Mary and Peter have invited us to a party on Saturday. Would you like to go, or are you committed to going to football?'

The response to the statement (a) is likely to be pretty hostile, whether or not both people end up at the party. The statement takes away personal choice, and the footballer is left having to fight their corner. They are under pressure.

The response to the question (b) is likely to be more positive. The footballer is choosing their destiny and may even decide to do both – on their own terms.

We talk to ourselves in the same way – often asking emphatic and negative questions that cause us stress and leave us fighting ourselves – rather than taking a more open-minded and questioning approach.

The assertive approach to beating stress

Assertiveness lies in the neutral ground between being passive and aggressive. Assertive behaviour is a powerful stress-busting tool because it is cool, calm, composed and honest. If you are able to be assertive you are able to be true to yourself.

An assertive response to stress tends to be:
❍ Composed.
❍ Relaxed.
❍ Confident.
❍ Direct and honest.

It will usually feature:
❍ Good eye contact.
❍ Steady, firm speech and a clear tone of voice.
❍ Active listening.
❍ The frequent use of 'I'.
❍ Relaxed and upright body language.
❍ A minimum of nervous gestures or movements.
❍ An even-paced voice with no 'ums' and 'ers'.

An assertive approach will maximize the chance of your message being well received and will also have a positive effect on how you feel about yourself.

Five steps to assertive problem-solving

1 Show the person you are speaking to that you understand their point of view by using phrases such as:
'I realize that...'
'I understand that...'
'I can see that...'

2 Say what you feel and think, perhaps by explaining the difficulties that their point of view causes you.
'I feel that...'
'I think that...'

3 State what you see as the best solution to the problem – and suggest how you can avoid it developing again.
'I want...'
'I'd like...'
'How about...?'

4 Ask the person you are speaking to for their response and reaction to what you are saying.
'What do you think?'

5 If necessary, reiterate what you have said, pleasantly but firmly, to reinforce your point:
'I understand that...'
'But as I have explained...'

Repeat as required, but keep a calm head and don't give in to angry criticism.

Assertive scenarios

In a situation where you are being put under pressure or feel you can't cope with another's needs, remember that you have a right to state your own needs too. Each of the following sequences follows the 5-step approach to being assertive (as on p. 107). Practise filling in the gaps and adapting the basic scenarios to suit your own requirements.

Positive thought:
'I have the right to say no.'

Assertive response:
'I realize that...'
'However, I feel unable to...because...'
'I would appreciate it if you would...or...so that I can...instead.'
'What would be the best solution for you?'

Positive thought:
'My opinion is equally valid and I have a right to be listened to.'

Assertive response:
'I recognize that everyone has...'
'I feel that my opinions have not...'
'I'd like the opportunity to...'
'Is that OK?'

Positive thought:
'I have the right to criticize in a constructive manner.'

Assertive response:
'I know that...'
'But I feel that...'
'I'd like to suggest that...'
'Do you agree?'

Positive thought:
'I have the right to be spoken to with respect.'

Assertive response:
'I realise that you are feeling...'
'However, I think that...'
'I'd like to...'
'Do you accept that...?'

If you are unused to stating your own needs or influencing others, it will take some practice before you are able to use the approach in every situation. Like all things in life, practice makes perfect. If it will help your confidence, try out the sequence in a shopping situation, or in a restaurant or other service-orientated environment, before tackling a serious work or social situation.

Change your mind, change your mood

When it comes to stress we are our own worst enemies. The less we feel able to cope, the more we bring stress upon ourselves. Every thought we have, every phrase we utter influences the way we think and the way we view the world and ourselves within it.

There have been scientific experiments to show the dramatic impact that language has on mood. Think back to your childhood and your time at school. Was there a teacher who made you feel that you could achieve and another who undermined your confidence? How did their language differ?

The lessons you learned at an early age are likely to have stayed with you. If you were told constantly that you were stupid, inept, could do better, or were likely to fail, you may still be talking to yourself in this way. If your parents were high achievers or had great expectations of you, you might feel the constant need to please and to perform. Failure is not an option for you because you will be letting people down. Negative language converts pressure into stress because you are constantly berating yourself and reinforcing feelings of powerlessness.

Equally, if you are in a relationship that has an unhealthy power balance or are working for a boss who has bullying tendencies, you may find that there has been a gradual erosion of your self-confidence and a steady increase in your levels of tension and stress. This will show itself in the way that you talk about yourself.

Take a look at the following phrases:

'I'll never be able to...'   'I'm hopeless at...'
'I'm so stupid.'   'I'll lose my job if...'
'It's not fair that...'   'There's no point in...'
'I should have...'   'Why didn't I...?'
'Everyone else is...'   'No one else ever...'
'What a shame that...'   'If only...'

'I wish...'   *'I can't cope with...'*
'I'll let everyone down if...'   *'I'm scared.'*
'I feel stuck.'   *'I feel so alone.'*

Are you feeling suitably depressed and demotivated now?
Your brain has just been bombarded with negativity. These
common responses to feeling overwhelmed contribute
nothing to our ability to overcome or manage stressful
situations. On the contrary, these negative messages
will reinforce your brain's understanding that you can't
manage, will lower your mood and add to your despair
and symptoms of stress. These phrases will make you feel
trapped, as if the walls are closing in. There is nothing
uplifting here that would help you envisage a stress-free life.

Negative or inappropriate self-talk leads to 'faulty
thinking' and a self-centred or exaggerated impression of
a situation. This sets the thinker up for failure. Passive and
aggressive behaviour feeds the thinker negative messages
about themselves.

To change your state of mind, you first need to review
the way you talk to yourself. If the habit of negative
language runs deep, this change of approach may feel
strange or artificial to begin with, but you need only
to read the following list of positive phrases to feel the
difference in the impact they have on your mind:

'I believe I can...'
'I have the skills and ability to...'
'I am enjoying myself.'
'I am learning from this.'

'In spite of...I will...'
'I choose to...'
'I will be able to...'
'I am motivated to...'
'My plan is to...'
'I will ask for...'
'I can take this one step at a time.'
'I am on top of this.'
'I will survive, even if...'
'Feeling fear is natural and the feeling will disappear when...'
'Failure is an inevitable stage in achieving success.'
'I am not alone.'

Positive thinking leads to positive talking and to a positive change of mood, literally. Our thoughts have the power to affect the functioning of our brain and our memory: the more you repeat positive messages, the stronger the message to your brain. (In the same way, negative messages are reinforced if they are repeated too often.)

○ Change your physical state by repeating positive affirmations as you breathe.

○ Change your emotional state by changing negative self-talk into positive self-talk.

○ Change your behaviour by consciously developing self-belief.

Three steps to positive thinking

1 Don't self-limit or pre-judge your behaviour. If you limit yourself by choosing to label yourself, you are likely to sap all your confidence before you've even tried to succeed.

Relax and make your stress work for you

2 Shape up your self-confidence by making a list of all your strengths, achievements, skills and experiences. Reading positive facts about yourself will help you to cope when you are feeling tired or stressed.

3 Keep the size of the problem in perspective (without diminishing its importance or relevance in your life).

Feeling stressed that you are going to be late for an appointment because of the level of traffic on the road is not going to solve your problem – especially when you left the house an hour later than intended and have brought the problem on yourself anyway. To take back control of the situation, you need to inform the person you are planning to meet that you will be late and must change the appointment time if possible. Don't be tempted to embellish or make grand excuses – keep it simple.

Body language and posture

Nothing speaks so well to the world about how you feel about yourself than your posture, and nothing says more about your mood and frame of mind than your body language. No matter how well rehearsed your positive phrases are and how upbeat the tone of your voice, if your body is giving those around you conflicting signals it will undermine your message. Your posture reflects emotion: the emotion that you are feeling and the beliefs that you hold about yourself.

Put this book down for a moment, then stand up as you would normally and observe how you are standing and how the weight is distributed in your body. Is your body telling a story that you're unaware of?

○ Putting your weight more heavily onto one leg and slumping slightly forwards and downwards with bowed shoulders is a sure sign of fatigue and dejection or low self-esteem. This is the 'flight' posture; you are trying to become invisible by avoiding eye contact and attempting to disappear.

○ A rigid and upright stance, with the neck stiff and the head slightly down, is likely to indicate a high degree of tension from worrying and being alert to danger. There is no sign of relaxation in the spine. This is the military posture: ready for fight rather than flight.

Any posture is potentially 'bad' for the body if it is held for too long. Your head weighs approximately 5–6 kg and is normally kept moving and in balance by the neck muscles, which are constantly contracting and relaxing. However, if you are repeatedly jutting your head forwards or holding it to one side, you will overwork one set of muscles and put strain on your spine. The more relaxed and alert you are, the more likely it is that you will have 'good' posture: upright, with the shoulders relaxed and slightly back, and with a slight hollow in the spine.

If you have neck or back pains, see an osteopath or find a good Alexander Technique teacher who will give you long-term preventative advice on improving your posture. A Pilates instructor or physiotherapist can also give you effective exercises and techniques to facilitate change.

'How you can help yourself – step 1', on p. 20, lists

several indicators of chronic stress and tension as it shows up in the body. I am repeating them here for ease of reference:

○ Hunched shoulders
○ Tightly-crossed legs
○ Crossed arms
○ Chewed lip
○ Neck spasm
○ Bowel problems
○ Shallow breathing
○ Nervous cough

○ Furrowed brows
○ Clenched fists
○ Tight jaw
○ Eye twitch
○ Lower back pain
○ Tension headache
○ Incessant yawning

Others symptoms include:
○ Ankle bending or tapping
○ Arms tightly folded
○ Nail biting

○ Coiled legs
○ Hair twirling
○ A gripped thumb

In general, gestures that close off the body from others, such as crossing arms or legs, are considered defensive and closed gestures; whereas uncrossed arms and a relaxed poise imply an open attitude. The more stressed you are, the more closed-off symptoms you will have – probably without realizing it.

Stop reading for a minute and pay attention to your body. Starting at your head, how tight are the muscles in your face, your neck, your shoulders? Are you clenching your jaw? How many of your limbs are crossed – and how tightly? Taking stock of how your body carries tension, several times a day, will also remind you of the importance of stretching, and relaxing, on a daily basis.

A brief word about muscles

Muscles work by contracting, and they do this in pairs. One set of muscles contract to raise your arm, while the opposing set of muscles contracts to move it back down again. If you are constantly holding your head or your body in a fixed posture, the muscles that are contracting to hold that position will become shorter and stronger, whereas the opposing muscles will become longer and weaker. Over time the body becomes unbalanced and you are more prone to injury. For that reason it is important to stretch and relax your body to overcome the tautness of tension.

Your stress and your children

Children are highly sensitive to your mood and the atmosphere in the home. If you are anxious, they will be anxious; if you are angry, they will be tense; if you are happy, they will be much more relaxed and joyful. Just as adults need reassurance that they are loved and safe for positive self-esteem, so children need plenty of affection and recognition of their worth.

If you introduce your child to the habits of relaxation and meditation when they are still at a young age, they will learn to use them as a matter of course in times of pressure and stress as they get older. Relaxation exercises are especially helpful to children who suffer from asthma or other breathing difficulties.

How you can help yourself – step 5: Think positive and speak out

Be aware

Think about the language you use when you speak about yourself to others. What sort of words and phrases do you use? Are they positive or negative? Empowering or depressing? Do they suggest you are in control, or being put upon?

Would you describe your choice of words as: positive; negative; apologetic; defensive; complimentary; self-deprecating; realistic or exaggerated?

Would you consider your tone of voice to be: downbeat; upbeat; neutral; undulating; passive or aggressive?

If you find this assessment difficult, ask someone you can trust to be supportive and constructive to describe your use of language and to tell you whether you tend to take a passive or aggressive approach to pressure.

Take action

Monitor your language to see how easily you fall into seeing the world as a glass 'half empty'. Each time you hear yourself come out with a negative comment, make a conscious effort to rephrase it in more positive terms.

❍ Angry that you feel put-upon at work? Decide how much of your workload you can reasonably cope with and speak to your manager or colleagues about redistributing the rest.

❍ Irritated by a neighbour's noise? Rehearse your complaint and express your concerns in a neutral and non-judgemental fashion.

○ Annoyed by company policy? Decide what you can do to influence the situation. Speak up, write a brief memo outlining your concerns – and if you can't agree, examine whether it is really the right work environment for you and consider alternative options.

○ Fed up with the lack of local transport? Write a letter or stand for local elections.

○ Depressed by the rainy weather? Plan to go somewhere or to do something that is not dependent on being out-of-doors.

I am not suggesting that you deny or suppress your feelings – it can be invaluable to cry, shout, use a punch-bag or do something physical to disperse the pain and hurt. Get the intensity of your feelings out of your system, and then take stock and plan your next move in positive language.

The point is, when we are feeling stressed there is a tendency to add to that feeling by seeing the whole world as negative or against us. Negativity and stress go hand in hand, because negativity implies that someone else is in control of your existence. In order to break free from stress you need to break the negativity cycle.

Conversely, beware of trying to be artificially positive in order to cope with a serious situation or tragedy. Denying your state of stress will not make the symptoms go away, it will just drive them deeper into the body.

Situations that are life-changing can be particularly challenging:

○ Looking after a chronically ill relative.

○ Adjusting to life after divorce or separation.

○ Coping with the ramifications of an accident or disability.
○ Discovering your child has been using drugs.
○ Moving house and/or job.
○ Financial problems.

All of these experiences and more will take their toll. In order to reduce the pressure and diminish any stress that these cause, you may need consciously to build or call upon your social or professional support network to help you through the worst times. Asking for help is never a weakness – rather it shows that you are assessing the situation honestly and choosing to manage it assertively.

Commit to change

Commit to the power of positive language. Commit to banishing forever the gripe or moan of dissatisfaction and self-pity. Practise using assertive language which will put you in control of the situation and enable you to speak up for your needs.

Commit, too, to being aware when things are out of control and you are near the edge of despair. A 'stiff upper lip' or 'pulling yourself together' attitude are not solutions. If you are feeling constantly tearful or desperate, you should not disregard or be ashamed of your reaction: you may be very near to breaking point. *Please* either speak to someone close to you, and whom you trust, about your feelings, contact your GP or seek a counsellor. Whatever you do, don't try to handle a difficult or challenging situation on your own.

Take back control
Getting to the heart of the matter

This chapter focuses on managing the causes of stress: primarily the ones that we bring upon ourselves through lack of self-care and lack of life-balance. Although tackling acute symptoms of stress is important in the short term, to bring about meaningful and lasting change it is critical that you also get to the heart of what is causing you difficulties and take some long-term lifestyle decisions that will allow you gradually to turn things around.

This chapter looks more closely at your personal stress-reaction style: your likely response to pressure, what motivates you to get out of bed in the morning and what you enjoy doing to unwind. It suggests options for action to help you create a personal package of stress-reduction techniques that will work because you'll be motivated to make them work.

Choose your approach

When you're in a state of stress your sense of proportion tends to go out of the window. You're likely to feel harassed and dejected with thoughts of:

○ I've got too much to do.
○ Other people have unrealistic expectations of me.

○ Nobody understands or cares.

○ I want to escape from this situation, but I can't.

It's quite common to find yourself repeating activities or habits that cause or add to mental or physical pressure. You may feel trapped or despairing and find that you are turning inwards on yourself so that you become unaware of or uninterested in the needs of others. Or the opposite may happen and you may be putting the needs of others so far ahead of your own that you're detached from your sense of self. When you are in a state of stress, life is out of balance and, for that reason, it can be helpful to take a whole-body (holistic) approach to changing your situation. Changing your physical state will change your emotional state and changing your emotional state means that you will be in a better frame of mind to take practical steps to change your situation.

We each respond to things in different ways, using a mix of physical, emotional and spiritual responses to the world around us. A key factor in stress management is relearning how to unwind. What are the things that make you relax, stimulate your mind, re-energize you? What is your relaxation style? What are you starving yourself of at the moment, and what would you enjoy that would make it feel as if life is back on track? At what time of day do you feel the most energetic and positive? Are you a 'morning' person or an 'evening' person? You are much more likely to change your current pattern of behaviour if you feel motivated to do something you enjoy and at the time of day when you are at your best.

The 'chill-out' factor

The following list is by no means comprehensive, but it gives a flavour of ways in which you can de-stress and rejuvenate the senses. Ideally, you will find activities that feed body, mind and spirit, rather than just focusing on one area in an unbalanced way.

Body

Activities that speed up the heart, get the blood pumping and raise your energy levels:

○ Keeping fit
○ Playing sport
○ Walking
○ Running
○ Cycling
○ Horse-riding
○ Yoga
○ Dancing
○ Diving
○ Decorating and DIY

Mind

Activities that stimulate the mind, teach you new things, encourage conversation and the company of others:

○ Reading and reading groups
○ Galleries
○ Museums
○ Classes
○ Drama
○ Learning

Relax and make your stress work for you

o Languages
o TV and radio
o Discussions
o Entertaining
o Time with friends

Spirit
Anything that lifts the spirit and heightens the senses in a way that makes you feel connected to the planet we live on and those around you:
o Music and singing
o Gardening
o Playing with children
o Loving relationships
o Creative activities
o Meditation
o Prayer
o Dance

These are not fixed categories, and there is overlap between the lists, but the ideal is to spend time enjoying things that stimulate all three areas of your being. In this way you will encourage a balance in your life and will enhance your health and sensual and spiritual awareness, as well as your social skills.

When your time is not your own

'That's all very well,' you may say, 'but I don't have time to do what I'm doing already, so there's no time for anything else.' If this sounds like you, start by taking a good hard look at the way you are currently dealing with your situation. You will probably need to revise priorities in certain areas to gain 'you' time, or you might need to pay someone to help you with basic tasks – if finances allow it.

If you're on the go from 6.30am until midnight, with no one to help you with essential chores, and if there is no one in your family who can help you out, consider paying a third party – or trading favours with a friend or neighbour – to free up some personal time. You might be weighed down by work and unable to keep on top of things; if so, make a case for some additional support at work and check that you are not inadvertently doing other people's jobs for them. One of the biggest causes of stress is lack of assertiveness and skewed perspective: an inability to see that there is another way of doing things.

Case studies: Getting help

Julie's elderly neighbour was pleased to take on occasional cooking for the children and even offered to do some ironing in exchange for weekend help with grocery shopping and for the enjoyment of being involved in family life. Julie also swapped baby-sitting nights with her friends Dan and Sandra – so she could have an evening out every fortnight. With the extra time she gained, Julie was able to take up yoga and to go swimming twice a week. Her renewed energy and fitness levels were exactly what she needed to cope with her pressures.

Mike had no free time at all. He arrived at work by 7.45 each morning and rarely got home before 10pm. He usually grabbed an evening meal, alone, at the local pub before commuting home.

His stress issues related to a backlog of admin work, which made him feel out of control and vulnerable to criticism from senior management, and also suffered personal isolation stemming from his lack of contact with friends.

It took a debilitating virus to get Mike to see life in a different way. During his time out through illness, he discovered that if he wasn't at work his junior staff picked up the admin work, and that if he stopped his frenetic pace his brain felt sharper. When he returned to work he promoted one of his team to become his personal assistant to take away the day-to-day detail and gave this person permission to organize him as much as possible. He changed his main meal to lunch, which gave him more energy and freed up his evenings for socializing, playing football and being more relaxed with his family.

Of course, it's not always that easy:

Val and Corin were both divorced with five children between them. Money was a major issue. Val had not worked full-time since she had had her first child, fifteen years ago. Corin was self-employed and based at home. Their debts were soaring and Corin's work was irregular. Val felt that their only option was for her to return to work. She was very nervous at the prospect, but it was a necessity. In the short-term Val's stress levels became worse, as she had to battle with the basics of learning to use a computer and the pattern of business life, before coming home to washing, ironing and chasing the children to do their homework. In time, however, as the money began to make a difference, she came to value her new-found role, looked into formal training and began to involve the children in running the house. The immediate result was that the children, not Val, brought Corin on board to help with the chores as well. Long-term result: their chronic financial problems continued, but they became a more unified and positive family.

Whatever your personal situation, if you can change your perspective to see a way to use your time differently, you are well placed to de-stress your life.

Stress caused by emotional pain or deep trauma

Time management will do little to improve your quality of life if your stress stems from a deeper underlying cause. If the pressures in your life are related to low self-esteem, depression, post-traumatic stress or family history, you may need some professional help to work through the effects of the past in a constructive and positive manner. Telling yourself to 'pull yourself together', or to 'stop being so stupid', will do nothing to ease the pain that is dominating your life and affecting the way you feel about yourself. Talking to friends and family could be immensely helpful – but may not help you to deal with the underlying issues, either fully or objectively.

In the further resources section at the end of the book there are brief descriptions of different healthcare professionals and how they can help. If the idea of talking about your problems to someone you don't know fills you with horror, or embarrassment, try looking at the situation with new perspective:

○ If you had a broken leg, would you go to a neighbour or to a surgeon?

○ If you needed to learn the principles of physics, would you go to a work colleague or to a specialist teacher?
○ If you wanted help in changing your image, would you go to your great aunt for advice or to a hairdresser or image consultant?
○ If you had a problem with a burst pipe, would you ask your best friend for help or phone a plumber?

Whatever it is that we need to know in life, we tend to ask for recommendations and to hunt down an expert in the field. Choosing counsellors, coaches and other professionals trained in behavioural and other psychological issues should be approached with the same rigour. If you have a good relationship with your GP and can gain a referral via your local healthcare trust, you may be able to save yourself some money as well.

Feeding stress

There are many ways in which we feed our own stress. Negative coping patterns include passive behaviour such as:
○ Doing everything yourself.
○ Not asking for help.
○ Rejecting help.
○ Saying yes when you could have said no.
○ Putting up with aggressive or bullying behaviour.
○ Assuming that things have to stay this way.
○ Drifting, rather than planning.
○ Not creating 'me' time.

Psychotherapist Vera Peiffer calls this 'the duty trap' (in her book of the same name): the denial of self that means you automatically put the needs of others ahead of your own. It may be that you feel guilty if you don't, or that there is no one else to ask. Some people are motivated from a deep-rooted need to be needed, or to help; while others may fear rejection if they don't put other people first. Alternatively, it may just be that you have been focusing so hard on trying to get things done that you have not realized that you have been neglecting important areas of your life. Suddenly, 'life outside' what you're doing seems to have disappeared, along with elements of your health and your self-confidence.

Recognizing that you need to do things differently is an important stage in de-stressing your life. The challenge is in the gap between knowing what you should be doing differently, and actually doing it differently. Old habits die horribly hard, even if they are self-destructive habits. Putting change into positive practice may be a struggle to begin with, but once you have time-bound targets for action in place – all you need to do is start. The first step is all-important. After that, the challenge is to keep going and to keep yourself motivated to stay on track.

'You always hurt the one you love'

Be aware of any signs of aggressive behaviour or abuse of yourself or others that might result from excessive stress. No matter how much pressure we are under, there is no excuse for taking our anxiety out on others who have no control over the situation. If you are constantly apologizing to your loved ones or feeling ashamed of your uncontrolled behaviour:

○ Recognize your actions as symptoms of stress.

○ Take time to identify the root causes of that stress.

○ Commit to changing these root causes.

○ Take time to unwind before you talk to those you are at risk of hurting (including yourself).

Managing other people's stress

'There's a good chance that the person you're helping already knows the solution to their problem. They just don't know that they know.'

SUSAN QUILLIAM

Stress doesn't just affect the person under immediate pressure; the ripples of distress affect those around him or her as well. Friends, family, work colleagues, neighbours, those at the sharp end in shops, on public transport and in hotels and catering all know how it feels to be on the receiving end of someone who has had a bad day. It can be very difficult and testing to try to help someone who rejects or denies the need for your help. Asking for help is often seen as a weak or feeble trait, so rather than ask for help in an upfront and direct way, there will be oblique hints and clues that all is not well. The signs may include:

○ Self-deprecating humour.

○ Negative feelings: being low, depressed, sad or constantly pessimistic.

○ Being ineffective: absent-minded, your mind is not on the job.

○ Escapism: an increase in drinking, smoking, eating, sleeping, drug-taking.

○ Clumsiness: being untypically accident-prone.

○ Uptight: being unusually irritable or nervous.

○ Self-neglect: dressing badly, lack of make-up, unkempt appearance, poor hygiene.

○ Hinting at problems: steering the conversation round to talk about your own issues.

○ Non-disclosure: 'There's no problem,' 'I'm fine.' Such replies tell you nothing.

If you are faced with the difficult situation of suspecting that someone is in need of help but you don't know how to approach them on this, the key is to become an effective listener, and to be patient. Ask them questions that show you care and are willing to help:

'Are you OK?'

'I've been a bit worried about you.'

'Is there anything I can do to help?'

'Would you like to have a chat over a coffee?'

'Is there anything you'd like to talk through?'

Such general questions have more positive impact than questions or statements that are judgemental or make assumptions. You may like to avoid the following:

'You've been looking pretty down lately.'

'You're having trouble coping, aren't you?'

'Shall I show you a better way to do that?'

'What are you doing that for?'

'Have you thought about going for counselling?'

'Would you like me to recommend a good hairdresser?'
'Why don't you...'

Avoid the temptation to lead the conversation by alluding
directly to the apparent problem or by offering unasked-
for advice. It is important that the individual takes
responsibility for and ownership of their own situation.
If they come to talk to you on their own terms, they will
be more likely to work towards a solution themselves.
Negative questioning may trigger a defensive response or
send the person into retreat.

People who have been trying to deal with excessive
pressure for a long time are likely to be holding a lot of
their feelings inside; they may not even realize fully what
the problems are. If you can allow someone the space to
talk and can actively listen to them, you will enable them
to 'find their own way' through the problem.

Active listening means:
❍ Asking 'open' questions that start with: *who, what, how,
where, when.*
❍ Listening without interrupting.
❍ Listening without directing what the other person is
going to say.
❍ Accepting the other person's point of view and the way
they are feeling.
❍ Not pre-judging the solution.
❍ Letting the other person find their way to their own
solution and in their own time.
❍ Not bringing your own agenda to the conversation.

o Keeping yourself out of the other person's way.

o Not taking emotional responses (such as crying or anger) personally.

o Not telling someone to 'cheer up' or 'snap out of it'.

o Being patient.

Inappropriate responses that make the speaker feel rejected include:

'I know what you mean. I had a similar experience...'

'Well, I told you ages ago that...'

'Look at it this way: it could be a lot worse...'

'I wouldn't do that if I were you. How about...?'

More appropriate responses would include:

'Tell me about it.'

'How do you feel about that?'

'There's nothing wrong in feeling that way.'

'Why do you suppose you feel guilty?'

Talking things through and helping someone to voice their thoughts out loud will enable them to:

o Change their physical response by speaking rather than internalizing.

o Change their emotional response by reacting to their voiced thoughts and feeling more in control.

o Change their behaviour by choosing to do something about it.

Being a confidant

Offering someone your support is a kind thing to do
– but it's not always appropriate. No matter how good a
friend or colleague you are, it is important to have a clear
understanding of your strengths and your limitations. This
is especially true in a family situation, where all kinds of
sub-agendas may be lurking without you being aware. If
you are already up to your ears in your own commitments,
trying to provide long-term support yourself may be
impractical. Short-term help in finding a more practical
longer-term solution may be more appropriate; but don't
overcommit yourself – if you let him or her down later, you
will both suffer.

Be clear about your reasons for helping. Do you
genuinely want to help in a caring but detached way?
Or are you in part just curious about the individual's
situation? Perhaps you have cast yourself in the role of
carer: you may want to rescue the person from their
troubles; or perhaps caring for others fills gaps in your own
life. These reasons do not necessarily preclude you from
being a supportive carer, but be aware of your own motives
so that you keep the needs of the other person centre stage.
❍ Be aware that you need support too, and that to carry
someone else's stress load is to increase the pressure you are
under as well.
❍ Make sure that the person who is confiding in you can
count on your discretion and loyalty.

Helping someone through a stressful period or a personal
crisis can be challenging, because it will inevitably progress

at their pace, not yours. Relationships psychologist Susan Quilliam tells the story of looking after her 6-year-old goddaughter who has fallen and hurt herself. Susan tries everything to make her feel better, and fails. She eventually asks the little girl what is needed to make her feel better. Her goddaughter replies: 'I'm *not ready* to feel better yet. What do *you* need to feel better?'

The wisdom of children! You cannot *make* someone feel better about themselves and you cannot *make* them change. All you can do is offer unconditional support and help them to be what they want to be, and to do what they want to do. Their choice of outcome will always be slightly different from what you would have expected.

For that reason it is important not to take the other person's response personally if they choose not to follow up on something you say or appear to reject your help. Helping is a two-way track and needs to take place amongst equals: if either party feels uncomfortable or patronized, the relationship will fail.

Stress changes as we change

What starts off as a high-pressure and stressful situation will not stay at the same level of pressure indefinitely, because once in the stress 'zone' (p. 33) we will adjust – either to a point where we are comfortably stretched and challenged or, on extreme occasions, to a point where a physical or psychological breakdown will force an adjustment and a change of pace (see pp. 40–1).

If your stress stems from positive pressure, such as having to adjust to a steep learning curve in a new job, there is every chance that the stress can be transformed into pleasure in time, once you have experienced success in your new role. Likewise, as we've explored in other chapters, a relatively low-level pressure, such as having a relative to stay, may develop into a more stressful experience if they outstay their welcome and their personal demands become overwhelming.

Emergency tactics

The reality is that we often feel at our most stressed when we are short of time and resources and when too many people want things from us *now*. If you've had it up to your ears with your children, partner, boss, domestic chores, and you feel you are about to lose your temper or cause someone some serious damage, you need to put distance between yourself and the situation – fast. Be aware enough of your feelings to keep things under control.

If you think you are about to lose your temper or feel you are about to cry:

❍ Remove yourself from the room with an excuse.

❍ Take deep breaths.

❍ Find something absurd in the situation that you can smile or laugh about (to yourself!).

❍ Distract yourself by thinking of something that is non-stressful: your cat, your child, the football match last week. (Or, if those are your stressors, choose something neutral: a sunset, a rainbow, a motorbike, running or travelling.)

We can usually raise our game to deal with one high-pressure situation, but coping with more than one stressful event is an immense challenge. The combination of such things as noisy teenagers, looking after a relative during convalescence, balancing the demands of the school holidays with a full-time job and running a house, or being apart from your partner for a long period of time, will take their toll. Whatever your core issues, don't underestimate their impact on you and your body. If you feel overwhelmed: *stop*. Bring in some help. Take a day off to recharge your batteries. The world will not come to a halt – but you might if you continue at your present pace!

Case study: The professional carer

Raj had been in the armed forces for much of his professional life and had seen active service at the front line. He had loved the camaraderie of the lifestyle and had risen to the rank of captain, but he lost an arm while in conflict and was forced to take early retirement. The horrors that he and his troops had witnessed refused to leave him, and he did not sleep well. He was much liked by those he met, but he found it difficult to relate to people on anything more than a superficial level. His disability made it harder for him to find permanent or well-paid work and so he began working in a sheltered housing complex for elderly people.

He was frustrated that the loss of his arm slowed him down; he had financial pressures, was unhappy with the noisy on-site flat he was living in and was lonely. He had been single for several years. He became increasingly isolated from people of his own age (37) and felt that his life was behind him. He didn't always eat a proper meal and was aware that he was drinking spirits on a regular basis, and alone at home. He felt tearful and began to have suicidal thoughts on occasion.

Personal perception

- ○ His life was over.
- ○ His disability made him unattractive to women.
- ○ Life was unfair.
- ○ No one understood.
- ○ He was tired all the time.
- ○ He was stuck in a dead-end job.
- ○ He would never be free of his war memories.

In spite of his private despair, Raj was attentive and caring towards the tenants in the housing complex. He became particularly friendly with Ken, a widower of 83 and a veteran of World War II. The older man recognized what Raj was going through and encouraged him to talk about the things he had experienced in battle. He was also able to tell Raj many stories of fellow soldiers with disabilities far more severe than his own who were able to make good and happy lives for themselves. In spite of their own horrific memories, they had been able to shed the weight of the pressure and stress of conflict in order to start looking forward instead of back. Initially, the stories made Raj feel even more of a failure, but Ken's gentle dignity and understanding began to act as a catalyst and Raj started to realize that he had to assimilate the past rather than let it dominate his future.

Altered reality

- ○ He was lucky to be relatively able-bodied and to have nothing more severely wrong with him physically.
- ○ Talking to Ken was more valuable than he had admitted – he realized that perhaps he did, after all, need to see a professional counsellor to help him overcome his self-destructive feelings.

○ It was in his power to move house and live somewhere off-site.

○ His brain was in good working order and there were other employment or self-employment options open to him if he wanted to pursue them.

○ It was his attitude rather than his disability that was keeping him single.

By changing his personal view of his situation, Raj transformed himself from being a victim of circumstance to a man in charge of his own destiny. The sense of achievement that he gained from that decision fired him up to continue on his new path of change and to keep up the stress-busting lifestyle outlined below.

Stress action plan

Immediate

○ A return to fitness by taking up running this week.

○ Place advert to find new accommodation by the end of the month.

○ A commitment to smarten up and be more sociable.

○ Call AA if the whisky bottle called in the evening.

○ Arrange social suppers on a weekly basis for the residents to encourage a healthy-eating habit and to stop their isolation too.

Longer-term

○ A return to education to retrain as a teacher.

○ A course of counselling with a cognitive therapist.

Break the stress habit

If you have suffered a series of shocks, such as bereavement, an accident, a relationship break-up, a job loss, it is important to recognize that you have been through a period of acute stress and that you may adjust in a negative rather than a positive way in the short term. Talking and being in the company of others is a crucial part of recovery. Feeding stress-fired depression with alcohol, smoking or other negative habits will delay recovery and make things worse. Doing without these crutches can be hard on your own, so don't be afraid to seek professional help if necessary.

The first time you become acutely aware that you are suffering from the symptoms of stress may be when you find yourself weeping uncontrollably for no reason, or when you are forced to make an appointment with your doctor because you are suffering from panic attacks or other clusters of symptoms. You may find that your usual programme of exercise or activity leaves you feeling weak and exhausted rather than energized and on top of things. Fatigue-related illnesses are frequently related to pressure overload and may result in depression.

To decide what you want to change in order to break the stress habit, ask yourself:

○ What *change* can I make that will prevent this level of stress?

○ What is the *best* thing that can happen if I make that change?

○ What is the *worst* thing that could happen if I *don't* make that change?

- Can I live with the *consequences* of success or failure?
- Do I *want* to bring about change enough to take the first step?
- *What* is that first step?
- *When* am I going to take it?
- *Whom* can I trust to help me take it?
- *When* am I going to ask for their help?

We have a tendency to rehearse our decisions in life. Rather than realizing that something is amiss and trying to improve matters, we may think about the options for change and then revert to current behaviours. Our present state of being, however dreadful, is familiar and so on some level it is comfortable. Deciding to change can in itself bring additional stress. Fear of the unknown can, in the short term, make the immediate crisis seem acceptable by comparison, so we therefore adjust to our current levels of stress and hope that things will get better.

And so the cycle continues, and the levels of stress continue. By the time the crisis point comes around again, you are even more deeply entrenched in stressful behaviour and the challenge of overcoming the obstacles has become even greater. The stress-filled behaviour has become 'the norm'. Every week, every month, every year, the cycle continues – until the pain and discomfort are so great that they threaten your long-term survival: impacting on your health, your identity, your relationships; or your future. Look back at the stress 'zone' on p. 33 – the pattern is easy to see.

When dramatic change eventually comes it often turns

Relax and make your stress work for you

out to be quite a simple decision. Stopping smoking, leaving a relationship, resigning from a job, going though with an operation – once your mind is made up, you will do it. In many cases your friends won't be surprised: 'You've been saying you want to start your own business for years;' 'You haven't been happy in that relationship for a long time;' 'I wondered why you hadn't put the house on the market before.' Whatever the scenario, it seems that we give away more than we think we do, and it is often the fear of change, rather than the change itself, that causes anxiety.

If you are aware that there is a cyclical pattern to your stress-related behaviour, it's time to be honest with yourself. Is your pressure triggered by a recurring event; at a particular time of year; by a particular person or people? What are the influences that take you to breaking-point? Once the moment has passed, and your pressure subsides, are you lulled back into a sense of secure complacency?

Sometimes our stress-related responses become a habit that remains long after the original source of the stress has disappeared – and so we keep working late, feeling harassed, shouting at the kids or drinking too much, even though the source of the original stress has been resolved.

If you suspect that you are contributing to an unhealthy pattern of behaviour, speak to someone you trust and ask them for their candid opinion of what you are doing. (But don't shoot the messenger if they say something you don't like, or didn't want to hear!)

Getting out of your own way

It is also worth mentioning our own role in causing stress – to ourselves and others. Sometimes we choose to adopt the role of carer, rescuer, martyr, workaholic, high achiever, perfectionist, idealist. There are times when these roles are positive and appropriate – but if we adopt them permanently, as a way of defining ourselves, we become complicit in causing the very stress we are trying to avoid. It can be quite a shock to discover that we are our own biggest problem.

There are some common signs and solutions:

○ If you find it hard to say no to requests from other people, you may have a problem with assertiveness. See p. 106 for tips on how to practise assertiveness.

○ If you have always been a high achiever you may expect yourself to be at the top of the tree on every occasion. The possibility of failure, or personal criticism, is too high-risk. If this sounds like you, see p. 158 for comments on perfectionism.

○ Acting more for other people's benefit than your own can begin at an early age, when decisions are taken for the good of your parents or teachers rather than yourself. As an adult this can lead to you being unsure of who you are, and continuing to act to please others. You may need to take courageous steps to face your fears and to learn more about yourself: perhaps by taking up a dance class, going on an outward-bound course, joining a drama group or going on a solo holiday.

How you can help yourself – step 6: Managing and monitoring your response to stress

Be aware

The brain tends to work best when it has a goal in mind. If every part of your being is focused on the same outcome, you will be less likely to give up when the going gets tough. You might find it most effective to have a target 'start date' for your new life pattern. Clear a weekend; ask your nearest and dearest to support you in your plans and buy yourself a diary, or a wall planner, or whatever will motivate you to plan ahead and keep track of your progress.

Before you get started, take a week to monitor closely how you use your time. Don't try to correct or alter your behaviour; just keep an honest tally of your movements. You will then be able to see a pattern emerging and will begin to understand yourself and your motivation more deeply.

When you're planning time to unwind, treat the time you are allocating to relaxation with the same commitment and dedication as you would something in your work or social life, or your children.

Monitor yourself closely

○ What time do you get up?
○ Are you a person of routine, or do you hate to be tied to time?
○ At what time of day do you feel most alert and energetic?
○ At what time of day do you feel slowest and sluggish?

○ Do you eat regular (and healthy) meals, or do you snack and graze?

○ Do you put off doing things you dislike?

○ Do you waste time when working because you'd rather be doing something else?

○ Do you sacrifice relationships for work, or vice versa?

○ Do you overcommit and try to do too much at once?

○ Do you work for long periods without taking a break?

○ Do you find it hard to settle and concentrate?

○ How long do you spend with friends or on the phone?

○ How much time do you spend watching TV?

○ What time do you go to bed?

Use your findings to decide which area of your life is your priority. If you tend to work long hours and flat out, think how you misuse your time to give yourself false breaks, such as social calls, web surfing or TV 'veg-out' to allow your brain a rest. If these feature in your day it would be more effective to give yourself a proper break to recharge your batteries so that you return to work more effectively.

Goal-setting

Which of the following best describes you?

A – I set goals in the workplace, but at home I take things as they come.

B – I set myself goals in every area of my life and try always to be the best I can be.

C – I have too many goals and too many conflicting pressures on my time. I find it impossible to keep up with them all.

Rather obviously, person A is likely to be the least stressed; person C the most stressed and person B may move from being under personal pressure to great stress depending upon how well they can handle not *always* being the best at everything.

In order to pin down the parts of your life that you have most control over at present, and those that you have least control over, take time to consider these different areas. It is useful to start off with general categories and then break them down into smaller themes so that you can really pinpoint where the problems lie:

Work
Working for someone else
Work colleagues
Location of work
Quantity of work
Deadlines

Relationships
Sex and relationships
Friends
Family responsibilities
Children

Health
Diet and nutrition
Fitness

Money

Your home

Resources

Debt

Retirement

Personal

Self-esteem

Self-image

Self-confidence

Quality of life

Fun and laughter

Time to oneself

Time with family

Hobbies

Holidays

Material possessions

Add any other categories that are relevant to your own life and situation.

Take action

For each category, consider the following:

○ Am I satisfied with this area of my life?

○ What would I like to happen in this area of my life?

○ What goals do I want to set for this area of my life?

○ Is the way I am living compatible with achieving those goals?

○ I don't feel as if I can control this area of my life.

○ I cannot control what happens in this area of my life.
○ I can control what happens in this area of my life.
○ I can slightly control this area of my life.

Look particularly hard at the last category. Have you got more choice and influence than you realize?

Take stock of your results and list the three most stressful aspects of your life right now:

1 _____
2 _____
3 _____

Think of *just one thing* that you could do in each area that would bring about a positive change. Do you feel confident that you can make that change?

Yes? Great. You can move on to the 'commit' stage.

No? Then take your time and consider something else that feels more realistic. It doesn't matter how small a change it is; any step towards taking control of your situation is a move in the right direction. Keep considering your three main challenges carefully until you have made a realistic assessment of what you can do.

Commit to change

In making a commitment to change you are setting yourself a goal. To monitor your progress, so that you can see how far you have come, it is extremely beneficial to keep a diary. This will help you to stay on track if you have a day that feels wobbly, or on occasions where additional pressure hits and you feel control has gone out of the window.

Make a date with yourself: perhaps at a weekend or on the first day of the month, or right now, if that's what motivates you. Schedule your changes into your diary.

For example, if lack of energy is causing you stress and you need more exercise, you may intend to get up twenty minutes early to go for a walk. If you know you enjoy a lie-in, schedule a 'going to bed' time that is half an hour earlier as well. This is harder than it sounds and needs thought, planning and practice, but it is part of the same process that brings about other significant changes.

Too much time at the office, too many deadlines, and not enough time at home? Plan in advance what time you are going to leave work. Schedule a reminder into your computer or tell a colleague if necessary. Alternatively, arrange to meet someone 10 minutes after you intend to leave work – and don't cancel! Work consciously instead of instinctively: decide at the beginning of the day what you are going to do, and stick to it:

○ Change your physical response by planning.

○ Change your emotional response by responding positively to the plan.

○ Start to behave differently and gradually regain control over each area of your life.

Keep your progress under review. If something doesn't work, don't give up; ask yourself, 'Why?', 'How?' and 'When?'. Why didn't it work? How could you have handled the situation differently? How could you have behaved differently? How can you regain control next time? When can you begin again?

The greatest feelings of stress stem from a sense of powerlessness: the feeling that others are pulling your strings; that you have no choice; that you cannot make your own decisions. The greatest cure for those feelings is to develop those areas where you do have choice so that they become larger than the ones that are causing you stress. If you can develop ways to manage the causes of your stress, you will develop a sense of control over your life as well.

6 Keeping on track
How to overcome setbacks

'Acceptance is, in fact, the first step to successful action...if you don't fully accept the situation, you will never really know if the situation should be changed.'

PETER MCWILLIAMS

If progress happened in a straight line, it would be easy to follow the strategies outlined in this book and to make steady and irrevocable progress onwards and upwards. Unfortunately, as we all know, life isn't like that. Excellent progress can be overturned in an instant by something that attacks the very core of our vulnerability. A chance remark, a memory flashback, a physical response to a challenging situation, lack of sleep or simply too much to face all at once can send us spiralling downwards; sometimes to a place that feels lower than where we started.

If you are finding that you are overwhelmed by symptoms of stress, take a look at the bigger picture. Just as your symptoms of stress crept up on you slowly, without you appreciating their true impact, so too will it take time to bring about lasting change to the way you manage your day-to-day response to the root causes of pressure and stress. Just as 'a journey of a thousand miles starts with a single step', so too your own journey starts with a single action: the renewal of your determination to get your life back on track.

Start where you are

Are external pressures grinding you down? Has the option of cool-headed planning gone out of the window? Are you overwhelmed with conflicting priorities? Has your health and fitness taken a downturn? Whatever your stress symptoms, you *can* overcome them. If you've done it before, you *know* that you can do it again; the key is to accept what is happening and look it squarely in the face.

○ First of all, stop what you are doing. Examine the week ahead and reserve a period of time away from the heat of the pressure. No matter how critical every minute seems at the moment, believe me, you will have renewed energy if you change your pace, and your environment, for a minimum of twenty minutes.

○ Take stock of the pressures in your life. What is at the root of the increase in your stress levels? Who or what is in control of you at the moment? And what is within your control to change?

○ No matter how overwhelmed you are feeling, it is possible to use your time and resources more effectively. Review p. 79 for ideas on how to plan ahead and prioritize.

○ Are you carrying too much on your own? Review Chapter 4 for guidance on how to ask for support and how to delegate – this will reduce the pressure on you and put you firmly back in control.

○ Take a look at your lifestyle and see whether your diet, exercise, relaxation time or other factors are out of balance

○ Breathe! If your body is holding a lot of tension you will increase your stress levels. See p. 20 for guidance on relaxation techniques.

○ Accept that you are experiencing a period of acute discomfort, but believe that things *can* change and can change for the better.

○ Do the exercise on pp. 146–7 to assess your core stress areas and choose to change your situation.

Remember that you always have a choice

'We who lived in concentration camps can remember the men who walked through the huts comforting others, giving away their last piece of bread...they offer sufficient proof that everything can be taken from a man but one thing: the last of the human freedoms – to choose one's attitude in any given set of circumstances.'
VICTOR FRANKL

No matter how great the level of stress we are under, we can still choose our response to it. The rush of adrenaline that comes to our rescue triggers the fight or flight response, but that in itself implies choice: to face the source of your stress head on, or to flee from it. Which route you choose depends on the source and the nature of the stress. You're unlikely (I hope!) to choose to stand in the road and fight with an oncoming truck, but you may choose whether or not to let your fear of a room full of strangers stop you from learning to dance, going to a party or giving a presentation.

Relax and make your stress work for you

Remind yourself that you *always* have a choice – even if it is only a choice of what kind of attitude to take (as illustrated by Victor Frankl's quote). Whether you decide to walk away from the source of your pressure or whether you choose to see a situation through, don't dwell on it for too long. To make a decision and to take some form of action is better than to take none at all. If you feel you could have behaved differently, take stock and resolve to act differently next time. Think of yourself as a child learning to ride a bicycle – you will probably fall off several times before you finally master it.

To put yourself back on track, remind yourself what you decided to change in order to break the stress habit, and what questions you asked yourself in order to make that decision (see p. 139).

It is one of the truisms in life that your close friends and family have probably intuited more about you and your life than you give them credit for, not least because you have probably been giving out messages in rehearsal for the changes you want to make months or even years ahead of taking the first step. (You can remind yourself of the cyclical pattern of stress that can develop before we finally plan for effective change on pp. 139-41.)

Your health is your priority

The phrase 'your health is precious' may sound like a cliché, but it is never more true than when your back is against the wall and you feel that your life is not your own. Your health and fitness need to be your number one priority when you are facing a period of chronic stress. If you can 'shape up for stress' you will be able to deal with its effects much more easily.

You know how you feel when you've neglected yourself: bloated, fat, sluggish and unattractive, or pasty, tired and suffering headaches or stomach problems. You also know (although you may have forgotten!) what you feel like when you have been looking after your diet and getting some exercise: energized, in good shape and positive about yourself.

If you tend to 'let yourself go' when you are under pressure, and you haven't got the time or resources to go the gym or a fitness class regularly each week, build exercise into your day in other ways. Walk instead of drive; run instead of walk; take a brief energetic stroll between tasks/meetings/appointments; play energizing music while you're doing household chores. If you have to fit time for exercise around the needs of your family, get them involved too: children rarely take enough exercise these days and a walk, a knockabout with a football before suppertime, or anything else that gets you moving and relaxing, will give you precious time with them and de-stress you as well.

If your worry takes a more obsessive/perfectionist form and you find yourself overdoing it at the gym, or being overconcerned about tidiness or your appearance, try taking up something less competitive and more relaxing, such as yoga, tai chi or chi gung. These forms of exercise will slow you down whilst also making you become more conscious of your body in a positive way.

Nourishing nutrition

Healthy eating is often the thing that disappears off the agenda when you are feeling stressed. If you live on your own it is all too easy to reach for the fast food or sweet-treat fix and forego real, healthy meals. Having a young family to feed may also increase the likelihood of you stocking up the freezer; but is it full of ready meals and frozen food rather than healthier, more nutritious options? Eating out is the easy choice for those who can afford it – but be warned, it may lead you into wine and dessert temptation, as well as put unnecessary pressure on your cash flow.

Without a doubt, we are what we eat. so, to optimize your chances of feeling energetic and minimize susceptibility to illness, try to cut down excessive intake of refined sugar, saturated fats and stimulants. If you concentrate on increasing the quantities of fresh fruit, vegetables and herbs in your diet, combined with moderate levels of protein and carbohydrates, you will find that cravings for 'stress foods' gradually diminish and you will not be held hostage to your stomach's whims!

It comes as a surprise to many to find that healthy food is as easy to prepare as, and can take only a little more time than defrosting and heating, a pre-packaged meal. Good nutrition takes a bit of planning, but it doesn't need to be time-consuming – many people even find that preparing a meal is a relaxing way of unwinding and de-stressing at the end of the day. There is any number of books on healthy eating and meal planning available, so I am not going to go into diet plans and recommendations here. If you're not used to cooking, take advice from friends who are keen cooks: buy a cookbook that is simple to use and caters for your tastes and likely food preferences; alternatively, consult a nutritionist for specialist advice on your personal diet. Put the emphasis on the principles of eating fresh ingredients as much as possible, and take seriously the recommendation of a minimum of five portions of fruit and vegetables each day.

The power of pampering

As anyone who has ever had an aromatherapy massage or a facial can verify, the power of pampering cannot be underestimated. Pampering does not have to cost you a fortune, and can be enjoyed as much in your own home as in a luxury health spa. Take half an hour to luxuriate in an aromatherapy bath; use scented candles; encourage your partner to give you a massage; treat yourself to a salon haircut. Remember too that pampering is no longer exclusively for women and that many men are discovering the benefits of massages, manicures or simply a relaxing bath. Treat yourself well and do something at least once a week that makes you feel good about yourself.

Set goals and priorities

If you have a clear idea of where you're going, what you're doing and why you're doing it, you will find that even if the pressure increases, the stress will diminish. Focus on the essentials and create a support network around you that can help with the rest. Concentrate on one thing at a time, and that way you won't be distracted from the main task or end up doing several things badly.

Don't be a martyr in your own home. Get others to help you with domestic tasks; if you have children, encourage them to play their part from a very early age by setting the table for supper, putting away clean dishes, tidying away toys, making the beds, folding dry laundry, and so on. This is not exploitation – it's teaching life skills.

Don't lose focus in the office. When under pressure there is a tendency to take refuge in the easier tasks on your list or to find yourself doing other people's jobs. Don't succumb to battling with a jammed photocopier instead of preparing for a presentation. If you need help, ask for it. Stay focused on your role and the bottom line.

Don't be afraid to ask yourself the 'big' questions. You only live once – you owe it to yourself to live your life to its optimum.

○ Are you happy with your close relationships and the direction in which they are going? If not, how could you improve them?

○ How do your closest friends make you feel about yourself and your situation? How do they affect your behaviour? Do you feel better when you are around them?

○ Could you use your working time more effectively?

○ Are you happy with the way that you use your free time? Or could you be doing other things that would be more satisfying?

○ Are you happy?

○ Do your life choices fit with your personal beliefs?

○ What are you willing to do to change your current situation?

Have realistic expectations

Perfection is usually considered to be something positive that we should aspire to; something that is superior to the majority standard. That we should keep striving until we achieve perfection is a common expectation; however, the problem is that perfection is not a fixed goal. No matter what we achieve, and no matter how well we achieve it, someone, somewhere, will do it better – eventually.

Those who are striving for perfection are doomed to living high-pressure and high-stress lives, because they are chasing a moving target. That is why so many high achievers undermine their own superb work with comments that it is hopeless or could have been better: perfectionists find it hard to be satisfied and always see flaws. As a result, perfectionists are in grave danger of suffering from symptoms of chronic stress. Perfection implies that you have achieved a final result, but in fact everything is in a state of perpetual change. We never achieve the final result, and so we are potentially primed for disappointment from the outset.

Time is often a major challenge for completing tasks. The more time there is to do something, the more we do, unless we have laid down a time-bound plan in advance. If you know that you find it hard to let go of projects, or that you give others a harder time than is fair if they don't do things your way, try to adopt a time-based solution to the perfection trap. The solution is usually based on the understanding that everything you aspire to achieve will be the best that can be achieved at a particular moment. Of course, it may be better in a few more moments, but if you have to draw a line, it will be perfect at that specific time.

This approach does not mean that you should compromize your standards or be content with sub-standard work. Keeping your standards high and your method of working efficient is important for self-esteem and personal growth, but there's no point in jeopardizing a deadline for the sake of non-essential details, or giving up life balance in pursuit of unachievable goals. Quality control and safety control are important, but an obsessive desire for perfection may itself be a sign of stress and a loss of perspective.

Case study: The lawyer

Neela trained as a lawyer. She was strong academically and was used to receiving praise and encouragement for her college grades. Her first job was as a legal assistant in a highly competitive environment working for a major commercial firm. Fast, willing and effective, she quickly became known as someone who performed well and would put in the extra hours to get the job done. As a result she was given more and more work, but in return she received little personal recognition and no increase in pay. Neela was struggling, both inside and outside work, but she didn't like to ask for help as she felt she should be able to cope on her own. Unable to manage her workload, she began to shun her colleagues' company after hours.

Within a year, Neela's reputation had diminished from

that of Wunderkind *to bottle-neck, from rising star to potential liability, from self-confident to highly stressed: she cried frequently, snapped unreasonably at the slightest provocation, and suffered from insomnia. Although only 25, she was becoming socially isolated and was* en route *for early burnout and a severe crisis of confidence. She decided to talk to a life-coach, who encouraged her to paint a picture of herself:*

Personal perception

○ *Too much to do in a day.*
○ *Put upon by senior management and colleagues.*
○ *Intelligent, and therefore should be able to cope.*
○ *Perfectionist, so no one else would meet her standards.*
○ *Used to praise. If she did something well, her boss would tell her.*
○ *Underpaid. If she was worth more, the firm would pay her more.*
○ *Not as confident as the others in the team – didn't fit in.*

In discussion it was discovered that Neela's problem was not so much the workload as her perception of her ability and what her rewards should be for the work she was doing.

Altered reality

○ *Her heavy workload was manageable but needed prioritizing.*
○ *Her lack of assertiveness and a fear of disapproval meant she was unable to find the right words to say no.*
○ *She was intelligent, but was hard on herself and lacked self-belief.*
○ *Being a perfectionist was not necessarily a positive trait – she lacked perspective and time management was poor.*

❍ *In a commercial environment good work is expected rather than praised.*
❍ *In a commercial environment increased pay has to be asked for and negotiated.*
❍ *Her colleagues had bonded as a group socially and were therefore more likely to share problems amongst themselves. She had not put effort into getting to know them.*

By altering her personal reality, Neela moved from feeling 'stuck' and like a 'failure' to seeing the bigger picture. She recognized that at 25 years old she had a lot to learn, that she needed to communicate her needs and achievements to her bosses in order to gain recognition, and that her social life also needed increased attention.

Stress action plan

1 Agree a set of priorities with her boss and team-members – and stick to them.
2 Practise negotiating and learn to say no when unreasonable demands are being made.
3 Put together a case for increased pay and promotion (based on results).
4 Get to know one or two colleagues and gradually reintegrate herself into the team.
5 Schedule time for friends and activities outside work.
6 Take time to relax – using relaxation techniques, by listening to music and, importantly, through physical exercise.

Give yourself a break

If you are working late for the umpteenth Friday in a row but have been invited to a friend's surprise party, ask yourself: 'What's the worst thing that would happen if I went home now? How much more work am I really going to do?' Get up a bit earlier on Monday morning to complete the work, rather than letting it eat into your leisure time.

Your work will benefit from this break as much as you will, because the brain is more effective and remembers more if you take regular breaks and open yourself up to a variety of experiences and new opportunities to learn.

The fear factor

Fear is probably your most significant obstacle to releasing your full potential. It can be an uncomfortable feeling, and one that most of us want to avoid, but fear is a natural outcome of the adrenaline response. Nervousness, panic attacks and all-out terror trigger the same physiological responses in the body.

The peculiar fact about fear is that it often changes its form when we look it in the face. Susan Jeffers, in *Feel The Fear and Do It Anyway*, says that: 'The only way to get rid of the fear of doing something is to go out...and do it.' The fear of fear itself and the feeling of helplessness that accompanies it are often more destructive and stressful than the effects or outcomes of confronting the source of the fear head-on.

If you are feeling fearful, don't suffer those fears alone, as they are in danger of becoming larger than they are. Fear is natural: it will make you feel uncomfortable, but in normal circumstances it won't kill you. If you can learn to absorb the discomfort and get used to the feeling, you will stop being so frightened of it and you will free yourself to try anything that you put your mind to. Remember that other people suffer fears too – even if they don't show them on the surface.

Case study: The intrepid survivor

Faith was a teacher in her mid-30s with no children. She had been physically active and independent all her life. She ate healthily, took exercise and had dealt effectively with the many and numerous pressures and challenges life had thrown at her over the years. Recently, Faith began to suffer numbness in her hips, legs and feet. The doctors encouraged her to have a thorough range of invasive and fatiguing medical tests. As usual, she dealt with it all with great determination and courage, until the day she received her results. The medical team delivered their verdict that Faith had multiple sclerosis, and that the situation could degenerate. Faith was inconsolable and became depressed, her fortitude collapsing as she envisaged a future of total dependence. She began to mourn her lost youth and her limited future and would burst into tears unexpectedly. She also cancelled social arrangements and confined herself to life at home.

Personal perception
○ *Life is over.*
○ *A future of dependence.*

O *Loss of independent action and movement.*
O *Reluctance to ask for help.*
O *No point in pursuing hobbies.*
O *Will be unable to travel.*

Faith was facing a form of grief: for the loss of her former good health and having to adjust to a new phase of life. She had always wanted children and now she saw that as a slim possibility. Anger at the 'unfairness' of life took over for a few weeks, but her depression was a vital stage prior to full acceptance of her situation, and, by accepting the stage she was at, she was able to make plans for the future and to find ways of compensating for her limited mobility.

Altered reality

O *Realization that she was limiting herself to a greater extent than was necessary.*
O *Awareness that her condition could go into remission and that having children was still a possibility.*
O *A desire to learn as much about the disease as possible in order to achieve optimum health.*
O *Awareness that she could teach anywhere in the world and still had the flexibility to travel if she managed her illness appropriately.*
O *Beginning to plan home adjustments for longer-term needs so that she could maintain her independence.*

Get enough sleep

Another effect of stress is that anxiety leads many people to suffer from restless nights and insomnia. According to Derk-Jan Dijk of Surrey University's Sleep Research Centre, 'By 3am we've usually had enough sleep to reduce our fatigue, and once that pressure is off, worries are more likely to wake us.'

This is a vicious circle, because lack of sleep in turn compounds feelings of daytime stress and vulnerability. Adults, like children, need a routine and a period of relaxation and winding down before going to bed. If lack of sleep is your nightmare, try the following sleep-enhancing techniques:

❍ Don't go to the gym, go running or take part in other sports activities in the late evening, as you will stimulate the body into action rather than encouraging it to wind down.

❍ Avoid eating a large meal or rich foods late at night. Your digestion does not stop when you are asleep and it will raise your body temperature, which may lead to restlessness or digestive problems. Foods such as red wine, cocoa, cheese and chocolate are common culprits.

❍ Resist the temptation to drink wine, spirits or cups of coffee two hours or less before going to bed.

Professor Colin Espie of Glasgow University's Sleep Research Laboratory has found that, 'When people wake in the middle of the night, they fixate on raking over the previous day and trying to solve tricky issues. It's a pattern that compounds the problem...because people become anxious when they are not awake enough to think straight.'

○ Keep a notebook by your bed and write down your worries if they wake you. The act of writing them down will release some of the tension in your mind and if you feel that you have addressed them you will start to relax and have a better chance of returning to sleep.

○ If you find that you are tossing and turning or lying awake for longer than 15 minutes, get out of bed and make yourself a warm drink. (Herbs such as camomile and valerian are said to be mildly sedative and relaxing and can be found in supplements or herb teas.) Breaking the tension by getting up can often be enough to help you fall back to sleep when you return to bed.

○ If you take sleeping pills, ask your doctor about how to come off them, slowly and over time. These pills diminish REM sleep and your ability to dream.

○ Do relaxation exercises in bed to encourage you to return to sleep.

○ Do a visualization that involves you falling asleep.

○ Sing to yourself silently, or recite lyrics or poems in your head.

Facing up to negative ways of coping

It is beyond the scope of this book to talk about the nature of chronic addiction or the underlying reasons for self-harm. It can be immensely challenging to face up to having a deep-seated problem or to help someone else to recognize theirs. The reasons behind an individual's addictive behaviour are likely to be deep-rooted and need to be tackled separately, away from stress-related problems.

However, if the behaviour is reasonably new and out of character it is likely that it is related to current pressure. If you are showing signs of unusually negative escapist behaviour, such as solo drinking, violent shouting, binge-eating, self-harm, excessive sleep – or even indiscriminate and obsessive TV-watching or computer-use – you owe it to yourself and others to find healthier ways to unwind. These bad habits do more harm than good because they erode your ability to cope as they use up your body's resources, compromise the immune system and leave your health at risk. If you feel things are getting out of hand, take steps to get help.

Don't cope alone

Extreme stress and chronic pressure are isolating conditions as you tend to cut yourself off from your friends through lack of time, money or other resources. If your social life is shrinking, lack of personal support may be one of your stress priorities on p. 147. In the words of John Donne, 'No man is an island,' and if you try to be one for too long you increase your risk of depression and other illnesses.

The power of laughter

Perhaps the most powerful coping strategy of all is laughter. Having a sense of the absurd is a wonderful barrier against stress. If you can laugh at something it loses its power over you and helps to change your perspective so that you see life in a new and different way.

How you can help yourself – step 7: See how far you have come and keep life in perspective

Be aware

❍ Remember that, no matter how bad your situation seems, you always have a choice. It may not be an easy choice to make, but the point is, you are always more in control than may first be apparent.

❍ Be aware of where you are in relation to the stress in your life. Have you got some areas of your life in balance? Give yourself credit for those areas that are positive and decide what you want to do about the areas that are problematic.

❍ Be conscious of your health and make sure your diet is healthy. Your physical body may well show the signs of pressure, even though you feel you are coping psychologically. Don't neglect early signs of ill-health and always make time to keep fit.

❍ Try to remember that, although feelings of panic and anxiety are uncomfortable, they are not in themselves life-threatening. If you suffer from feelings of nervousness and panic, use the breathing exercise on p. 20 to relax and to change your physical response to the situation.

Take action

❍ Setbacks to progress may sometimes feel more overwhelming than the original problem. This is partly because you know how much effort it has taken to bring about change to date; or it may be because your resilience is low and you feel as if no progress has been made at all.

❍ Setbacks do happen and, in order to plan for them, a

stress log or diary can be very useful as a way of keeping track of your progress. It will enable you to take a realistic look at all you have achieved to date, and stop you from repeating old patterns of behaviour – because by reviewing past actions you will see them coming in advance.

○ Measure your progress by following the steps outlined in Chapters 1–7: visualize, have self-belief, plan, prioritize, make your goals time-bound and measurable, communicate, review.

Commit to change

○ Commit to believing in yourself and to accepting who you are. One of the greatest causes of stress is the feeling that you have let others, or yourself, down. Before you can overcome the effects of stress you need to accept, wholeheartedly, who you are and how you came to be at this point in your life; you will then have a much stronger chance of achieving the future you envisage for yourself.

○ Commit to looking your fears in the face and, within reason, confronting them in order to move forwards. Fear is a large barrier to achieving potential; if you can keep your fear, and your challenges, in perspective, the future will be yours for the taking.

○ Commit to trying the 7 steps to beat stress. By taking focused and conscious steps to alter your reactions to stress you will be in a stronger position to manage challenges and cope with all that life throws at you. Have courage, and trust your ability to cope. We are each stronger, and have a greater capacity to cope, than we can imagine.

7 Back from the brink
Emergency action to avoid breakdown

When panic hits it can be hard to see the wood for the trees, and harder still to believe that things will ever get better. If you feel an overwhelming sense of panic coming on, focus hard on the three stages of change:

Be aware of your physical reaction.
Take action to change your reaction.
Commit to changing your approach.

Breakdown may last for a few hours, or for some people it may be a state that continues for several years; however, it always leads to radical life changes – and often for the better. If you are fearful of breaking down, practise the following techniques so that they become second nature to you:

○ Breathe deeply. Relax your body. Starting at the neck and shoulders, and moving through every limb of your body, contract and relax each set of muscles to get rid of some of the tension you are carrying.

○ Accept what is happening to you. Face your fear head on and tell yourself that the symptoms on their own cannot harm you or kill you. Tell yourself that the sensation cannot continue indefinitely. It *will* go away.

○ Avoid being tempted to feel sorry for yourself: the 'poor me' syndrome will only delay recovery. Acknowledge that you are feeling that way and don't feel guilty about it; but try not to let the feelings consume you.

○ If you find yourself overtaken by tears, let them do their work. Cry yourself to sleep if necessary, but tell yourself that just as the sun sets, so it rises, and tomorrow really is 'another day' and another start.

○ Don't waste time on 'if onlys' and 'what might have beens'. You can't change the past; only the future.

○ Keep busy. The more active you are, the less time you will have to focus inwards on your anxiety, and the better it is for your brain and body.

○ Think of at least one thing that it is in your power to change and focus on how that can be done differently.

○ Don't give yourself a hard time if your memory is out of kilter and your energy levels are low. In times of stress you are out of balance and overworking your immune system, so it *will* take time for you to recover.

○ Keep an eye on your progress. The more you understand about your personal responses to stress and pressure, the better able you will be to manage your future.

○ Don't experience panic and breakdown alone: phone a friend; phone the Samaritans; phone your GP. The simple act of taking action will move you further away from all-out panic. *You don't have to face it all on your own.*

In crisis

If you are with someone else who has lost control and is close to an emotional (and possibly physical) edge, the most important things to do are to remain as calm as possible and to focus on composed, reassuring communication.

○ Use the person's name a lot in your conversation: this will remind them who they are and that you are a friend and offering support.

○ Use friendly eye-contact to reassure them and help them to connect with you.

○ If necessary, go for a walk and get some fresh air/a change of scene.

○ Listen to what they have to say, but try not to let it become a repeating pattern.

○ If they are very distressed, focus on deep, slow breaths to calm them down.

○ Encourage them to talk about what is going on in the present, as well as what might happen in the future.

○ If the person is either extremely exhausted or high on drugs or drink, suggest that sleep is the best thing and that you can talk about it more in the morning.

○ Don't try to cope with more than you can handle. If medical help is needed, pick up the phone and get professional support.

Most important, stay with the person who is suffering and accept what they are going through. Don't try to judge them or cure them: just be there and let them know you care and you understand.

Conclusion

A breakdown is not an inevitable result of stress and anxiety, but a feeling of being close to breakdown or a sense of being unable to cope any longer will be familiar to many people reading this book. In order to avoid the possibility of breakdown, the most important thing you can do is to talk to someone or be with someone whom you trust – and who will not judge you. Using your sense of humour is a great way of cutting problems down to size too – and it will also help others to help you to keep things in perspective.

Although some of the suggestions in this book might seem fairly tough in terms of self-management techniques, it is important not to be tough on yourself as a person. Try not to blame yourself for your feelings or to berate yourself if you believe you have let yourself or others down. The chances are that you haven't – and that others will not judge you as harshly as you are judging yourself.

Most people experience a period of time during which they feel that they have lost their way or become overwhelmed by certain aspects of their life, and the majority of these same people will acknowledge that the self-knowledge they gain from these episodes does eventually contribute to their future in a positive way.

Step 1: Relax and live

○ Be aware – of your body's stress signals.

○ Take action – by controlling your breathing.

○ Commit to change – by practising relaxation techniques daily.

Relaxation is the key to beating your stress, and is the first step to releasing your true potential. By relaxing, you change your physical state and are able to control your emotions. If you can control your emotional responses you can also choose your behaviour and begin to manage the pressure you are facing.

Step 2: Face your fears and visualize the future

○ Be aware – of the true causes of your stress.

○ Take action – by looking at the facts, your feelings and your choices of action.

○ Commit to change – by starting where you are, and by drawing up a plan for change.

Once you have given physical form to the causes of your stress, you will begin to regain control of your life. The second stage in releasing your potential is to face your fear and choose a goal.

Step 3: Your stress, your choice

○ Be aware – of your reaction to stress and your symptoms of stress.

❍ Take action – by focusing your use of time and taking a problem-solving, goal-orientated approach.

❍ Commit to change – by changing your mind-set to positive and choosing to get fit and stay fit.

Permanent and positive change begins in the mind and managing stress is the process of planning your response to stressful situations, making sure that problems are not able to become larger than they really are.

Step 4: Shape up your life, your mood and your food

❍ Be aware – of the impact your stress-related mood may have on others.

❍ Take action – change to a time-bound approach to prioritizing tasks and add momentum and clarity to your day.

❍ Commit to change – by focusing on eating healthily as well as using your work time in a balanced and healthy way.

Planning and prioritizing are the keys to living a more balanced lifestyle, and if you are feeling calm and de-stressed, those around you will be affected in the same way too.

Step 5: Think positive and speak out

❍ Be aware – of the style of language you use to talk to yourself and others.

❍ Take action – to change negative-speak into positive-speak.

❍ Commit to change – and the power of positive language. The more you can state what you need in a calm and assertive manner, the less stress you will experience. Finding your own voice is an important part of stress management. Changing negative self-talk into positive self-talk, and ensuring that your body language is speaking as positively as your words, are important tools for communicating what you want and what you need.

Step 6: Managing and monitoring your response to stress

❍ Be aware – of your personal start date for change and stay focused on your goal.

❍ Take action – to decide which areas of your life are the top priority for stress-management and change and choose just one thing in each instance that you can improve right now.

❍ Commit to change – by starting a stress-monitoring diary, so you can chart your progress objectively on a day-to-day basis.

Setting personal goals and monitoring your progress by means of a written log or diary are the perfect way to keep yourself in control, positive and on track. It doesn't really matter how big or small your achievements are, provided you feel good about them and they help you to continue to move in a positive direction.

Step 7: See how far you have come and keep life in perspective

❍ Be aware – that you are always in a position of choice, no matter how stressful the situation.

❍ Take action – when you are confronted by setbacks.

Be determined and face up to your challenges; you will develop much greater self-esteem and respect as a result.
○ Commit to change – by believing in yourself and what you have achieved. Confront your fears and free up your true potential. You are much stronger and more resilient than you ever realized.

To achieve a goal you will need to follow each of these seven steps and monitor yourself carefully and honestly. Face your fears, stay on track, be kind to those around you and you will have much greater chance of keeping stress in perspective and developing to your maximum potential.

Your physical resources
○ Relaxation and breathing.
○ Healthy eating.
○ Exercise.

Your behavioural resources
○ Time management, planning and prioritization.
○ Assertiveness.
○ Communication skills.

Your social resources
○ Balancing home and work.
○ Building your social-support network.

Where to go for help and who does what

The information that follows will provide basic details about the main sources of help and treatment for stress and other related problems. For advice on how to find and select a qualified practitioner, please contact the regulatory bodies or associations listed on pp. 186-7.

Cognitive behaviour therapy (CBT)

Cognitive behaviour therapy focuses on the connection between what you think about yourself or a situation and how you choose to react to it. CBT takes a 'here and now' approach that focuses on causes and effects in the present day, rather than delving into your past.

The aim of CBT is to break cycles of negative thinking and behaviour, and to help you to cope more effectively with life by improving your self-esteem and self-image.

The CBT approach is action-orientated. With your therapist, you will draw up time-bound and specific goals that you would like to achieve – together with the strategies you need to put in place to achieve those goals.

CBT is used by specially trained and qualified professionals, such as clinical psychologists, psychiatrists and counsellors. Your GP or a mental health professional may be able to refer you to an appropriate therapist.

If you choose to consult a cognitive behaviour therapist privately you can find a qualified professional or check their qualifications via the British Association for Behavioural and Cognitive Psychotherapies (see p. 186).

Coaching

A coach is a facilitator, listener and motivator, whose role is to help the client to decide on their aims and ambitions, put in place achievable goals, and provide ongoing support to encourage the development of personal skills and self-belief to achieve those goals. Coaching differs from counselling and psychotherapy in that the relationship is driven by the client and focuses on practical outcomes, rather than addressing any deep-seated issues relating to depression, low self-esteem or poor motivation.

A coach is unlikely to share the same professional background as their client, but will use observation and questioning techniques to help the client develop their own solutions. Coaches are committed to remaining supportive and non-judgemental at all times.

Coaching may be the ideal solution if you need help in refocusing your goals and ambitions and have problems with prioritizing and personal motivation. Further information about the coaching process can be found on the Coaching and Mentoring Network website (see p. 186).

Complementary medicine and holistic therapies

Complementary medical practices are fully regulated, traditional disciplines such as acupuncture, homoeopathy, herbal medicine, osteopathy and chiropractic, which require many years of professional training. The techniques can be very effective for helping to reduce the

physical impact of stress, and can usually be used alongside conventional medicines (although you should always
inform both your GP and your complementary practitioner
of other treatments or medicines you are taking).

Holistic therapies, such as yoga, aromatherapy
massage, reiki healing, reflexology, t'ai chi and chi gung,
are invaluable for relaxing and balancing the energies
of the body. Some therapies include a spiritual element,
which can be immensely helpful to those seeking a greater
sense of meaning in life, although not essential in order to
benefit from the treatment.

The British Complementary Medicine Association will
help you to make informed decisions about what is right
for you. See p. 186 for contact information.

Counselling

Counselling involves talking one to one, and in complete
confidence, with a trained professional, who will give
you their full attention and commitment to help you to
transform your stressful situation into something more
positive. For those who are at a personal crossroads and
don't know which way to turn, working with a counsellor
can be invaluable, whether problems relate to everyday
concerns or deeper, long-term issues. Counselling should
be a personal and voluntary decision that is never forced.
To be effective it requires the complete commitment and
involvement of the client as well as the counsellor.

The counsellor aims to understand difficulties from
the point of view of the client by using active listening
techniques, enabling the client to understand the problem

from a different perspective. Trust in the counsellor is vital for the client in order that they feel able to express feelings such as anger, anxiety or grief, and get past any sense of embarrassment about showing their emotions.

There are various types of counselling including:

o Cognitive behaviour therapy (CBT) – see above
o Relationship counselling
o Counselling based on your personal faith
o Co-counselling – based on a system of mutual support
o Addiction counselling – for specific substance addiction

The British Association for Counselling and Psychotherapy can advise on how to select a qualified counsellor near you. See p. 186 for contact details.

Medical advice

Your GP or health centre will be a very good source of support and initial advice on how to manage the effects of stress or other issues relating to mental health. Your doctor may check your blood pressure and your cholesterol levels and make general recommendations concerning diet, exercise and lifestyle. It may also be possible to be referred for counselling via the NHS, or to get other specialized help. Prescribed medicines may also be recommended as either a short-term or long-term solution, depending on the severity of the symptoms.

For those who are reluctant to consult their GP in the first instance, NHS Direct is an excellent source of information and advice (see p. 186 for contact details).

Mentoring

Mentoring is similar in approach to coaching (see above), but a mentor is likely to be from the same professional background as their client and may well be working on a voluntary basis within an organization. A mentor's aim is to support their client and to help them to achieve their potential by enabling them to set and achieve appropriate goals, and offering the benefit of their own experience.

If your symptoms of stress are related to performance issues at work, the mentoring approach may well be the best solution as it can tackle the problem at source.

If you have deeper issues relating to low self-esteem, it could be valuable to seek counselling support as well. Contact the Coaching and Mentoring Network (see p. 186).

Neuro-Linguistic Programming (NLP)

NLP has its roots in psychology and neurology. It is concerned with how the brain works, the different ways we each process information, and how the brain can be trained to improve learning ability and positive well-being. NLP is used as an effective way of changing negative thought processes into positive ones, and can be used as a valuable technique to improve communication skills.

The Association for NLP International (ANLP) provides further information and advice on where to find a practitioner. See www.anlp.org.

Psychotherapy

There are many different types of psychotherapy, all of which have been developed to help people overcome stress, emotional or relationship problems and other mental health issues. All are 'talking treatments', but, unlike psychiatry, do not rely upon medication.

Psychodynamic psychotherapy focuses on past experiences and how these impact on feelings we have about other people. If problems are long-standing, treatment may take many months.

Behavioural psychotherapy focuses more directly on changing patterns of behaviour. It includes aversion therapy and desensitization techniques, which involve spending time doing or being with those things that cause anxiety. It is especially effective for anxiety-related conditions and phobias – and results can be immediate.

Family and Marital Therapy focuses on relationship problems by looking at the separate relationships between each of the people involved.

See also *Cognitive Behaviour Therapy (CBT)*, above.

A combination of these techniques may be used.

In individual psychotherapy, client and therapist talk one to one. In group therapy, several people with similar problems meet with a therapist. The impact of discovering you are not alone with your problem can be powerful.

See your GP or consult the British Association for Counselling and Psychotherapy for further information. Contact details are on p. 186.

Self help

There is an enormous variety of self-help groups in most communities these days. Each will have its own agenda and way of operating. If you are feeling isolated or you need some moral support, a self-help group may be the answer. Ask your GP for recommendations.

There is also a wide range of self-help books, tapes and CDs on the market. Reading about the issues that you are facing can be an excellent way of adjusting perspective and gaining an understanding of the situation and the future options available to you. Most bookshops now have a self-help section, but, if you would rather buy from the privacy of your own home, buying online is the ideal solution.

The self-help charities all have excellent websites that provide a range of practical and insightful information about stress-related conditions and how to manage them.

Spiritual health care

Spirituality is a deeply personal matter, which for many is associated with 'a deep-seated sense of meaning and purpose in life, together with a sense of belonging. It is about acceptance, integration and wholeness.' The Royal College of Psychiatrists recommends that 'A routine daily practice involving three elements can be helpful:

○ Regular quiet time (for prayer, reflection or meditation);
○ Appropriate study of religious and/or spiritual material;
○ Engaging in supportive friendships with others sharing similar spiritual and/or religious aims and aspirations.'

Spirituality differs from religion in that it is seen as extending across all creeds and cultures, while at the same time being intensely personal. Advice is available from religious organizations, complementary health centres, health food stores and on the internet.

Professional Support

Stress management
BBC health pages
www.bbc.co.uk/health

Centre for Stress Management
www.managingstress.com

The Coaching and Mentoring Network
Tel: 0870 733 3313
www.coachingnetwork.org.uk

The Happiness Project
www.happiness.co.uk

Life coaching
www.fionaharrold.com

No Panic
www.nopanic.org.uk

International Stress Management Association
Tel: 07000 780430
www.isma.org.uk

Health
NHS Direct
Tel: 0845 4647
www.nhsdirect.org.uk

British Complementary Medicine Association (BCMA)
Tel: 0845 345 5977
www.bcma.co.uk

British Heart Foundation
Tel: 020 7935 0185
www.bhf.org.uk

General
National Association of Citizens Advice Bureaux
Tel: see local telephone directory for nearest centre
www.citizensadvice.org.uk

Financial problems
National Debt Line
Tel: 0808 808 4000
www.nationaldebtline.org.uk

Counselling
British Association for Behavioural and Cognitive Psychotherapies (BABCP)
Tel: 01254 875277
www.babcp.org.uk

British Association for Counselling and Psychotherapy (BACP)
Tel: 0870 4435 252
www.counselling.co.uk

Relationships
Relate
Tel: 0845 456 1310
www.relate.org.uk

Sole parenting
Gingerbread
Tel: 0800 018 4318
www.gingerbread.org.uk

Addictions
Al-Anon Family Groups
Tel: 020 7403 0888

Alcohol Concern
Tel: 020 7928 7377
www.alcoholconcern.org.uk

Alcoholics Anonymous
Tel: 0845 769 7555
www.alcoholics-anonymous.
org.uk

Eating Disorders Association
Tel: 0845 634 1414
www.edauk.com

Narcotics Anonymous
Tel: 0845 373 3366
or 020 7730 0009
www.ukna.org

Quitline
Tel: 0800 002200
www.quitnet.com

Depression and Mental Health Care
Cruse Bereavement Care
Tel: 0870 167 1677
www.crusebereavementcare.
org.uk

Depression Alliance
Tel: 0845 123 23 20
www.depressionalliance.org

MIND – National Association for Mental Health
Tel: 0845 766 0163
www.mind.org.uk

Samaritans – 24-hour emotional support line
Tel: 0845 790 9090 (UK)
1850 609090 (RoI)
www.samaritans.org.uk

Bibliography

BBC Learning, *Managing Time – Trainer's Guide*, BBC Worldwide Ltd (London), 2002.

BBC Learning, *Putting Stress to Work – Trainer's Guide*, BBC Worldwide Ltd (London), 2002.

British Heart Foundation, 'Stress and your heart', BHF (London), 2004.

Buzan, Tony, *Embracing Change*, BBC Books (London), 2004.

Buzan Tony, *The Mind Map Book*, revised edition, BBC Books (London), 2003.

Candappa, Rohan, *The Little Book of Stress*, Ebury Press (London), 1998.

Courteney, Hazel, *What's the Alternative?* Boxtree (London), 1996.

Froggatt, Wayne, 'Twelve rational principles', www.managingstress.com/articles/froggatt.htm, 1997.

Holford, Patrick, *The Optimum Nutrition Bible*, Piatkus (London), 1997.

Jeffers, Susan, *Feel the Fear and Do It Anyway*, Arrow (London), 1991.

Kenton, Susannah and Leslie, *Endless Energy*, Vermilion (London), 1993.

McBride, John, and Nick Clark, *20 Steps to Better Management*, BBC Books (London), 1996.

Madders, Jane, *Stress and Relaxation*, Optima (London), 1979.

Marsden, Kathryn, *All Day Energy*, Bantam (London), 1995.

Norfolk, Donald, *Farewell to Fatigue*, Pan Books Ltd (London), 1985.

Peiffer, Vera, *The Duty Trap*, Element (Shaftesbury), 1996.

Rashani, 'There is a brokenness', (source and date unknown), as quoted on www.allspirit.co.uk/nondualquotes9.html.

Quilliam, Susan, *The Samaritans Book of What to Do When You Really Want to Help But Don't Know How*, Transformation Press (Brentwood), 1998.

Sample, Ian, 'Night of a thousand sighs' in 'Work', p. 3, *Guardian newspaper*, (London), 26 November 2005.

Weekes, Dr Claire, *Self Help for Your Nerves*, Thorsons (London), 1977.

Relax and make your stress work for you

Williams, S., *Managing Pressure for Peak Performance*, Kogan Page (London), 1994.

Williams, Stephen and Susan Iacovou, *The Pressure's On – Trainer's Guide*, BBC Worldwide Ltd (London), 2002.

Wilson, Paul, *Calm For Life*, Penguin Books (London), 2000.

Wright, Quentin, 'Starting over', *Saga Magazine*, p. 76, (Folkestone), July 2005.

www.quotationspage.com

Index